Looking, Making and Learning
art and design in the primary school

Bedford Way Series
Published by Kogan Page in association with the Institute of Education, University of London

Some new titles:

Personal and Social Education: Philosophical Perspectives

Reforming Religious Education: The Religious Clauses of the 1988 Education Reform Act

Financial Support for Students: Grants, Loans or Graduate Tax?

Looking, Making and Learning
art and design in the primary school

Edited by Anthony Dyson

Contributors:
Roy Prentice, Gillian Robinson, Gillian Figg,
Vera Coghill, Ken Baynes, Keith Gentle,
Sheila Paine, Anthony Dyson

Bedford Way Papers 36
INSTITUTE OF EDUCATION
University of London

First published in 1989 by the Institute of Education, University of London, 20 Bedford way, London WC1H 0AL.
Distributed by Kogan Page Ltd., 120 Pentonville Road, London N1 9JN

Typeset by Direct Design (Bournemouth) Ltd., Printers, Poole, Dorset.
Printed and bound in Great Britain by Billing and Sons Ltd, Worcester and London.

British Library Cataloguing in Publication Data
Looking, making and learning : art and design in the
    primary school. – (Bedford Way papers; ISSN 0261-
    0078; v.36)
    1. Great Britain. Primary schools. Curriculum
    subjects : arts. Teaching
    I. Dyson, Anthony, *1931–*   II. Prentice, Roy.   III.
    University of London *Institute of Education*   IV.
    Series
    372.5'044'0941

    ISBN .i.0-85473-312-4

Contents

Page

Editor's Preface
Anthony Dyson   vii

Some Recent Influences and Directions
Roy Prentice   1

Stimulus for Art in the Primary School:
an historical perspective
Gillian Robinson   12

Towards a Curriculum Model for Primary Art,
Craft and Design
Gillian Figg   33

Making and Playing, the Other Basic Skills:
design education for the early years
Vera Goghill   56

The Basis of Designerly Thinking in Young
Children
Ken Baynes   70

Direct Sensory Experience as the Source of
Nourishment for Ideas, Concepts and
Imagination
Keith Gentle   86

The Role of Humour in Children's Drawing
Experience
Sheila Paine   **98**

Learning About Art
Anthony Dyson   **110**

List of Illustrations

2.1 Seven-year old's drawing from direct observation, with the aid of a magnifying glass 22

2.2 Seven-year old's painting, enriched with crayon 24

2.3 Nine-year old children's drawings in response to
2.4 electronic sound sequences 25

2.5 Illustration by Robert, aged 8, to his own story 26

2.6 Robert's drawing (right) compared with one by Joan Miro 27

2.7 Nine-year old girl's picture, painted after studying Van Gogh's 'Crows in the Wheatfields' (1890) 30

3.1 Experimenting with various kinds of brush 42

3.2 Preliminary work for children's drawings of each other 45

3.3 Learning to look: pencil drawing from close and careful observation 45

5.1 Work by Welsh primary school children that involved
to close observation and critical analysis of existing
5.4 buildings and making proposals for a new building to fill a gap in the High Street (Art and the Built 78 Environment project: Cwmrhydyceirw and Ynstawe & Primary Schools, West Glamorgan 79

6.1 Playing on the beach 88

6.2 Vehicle building and testing 96

7.1   Drawing at four years, Charlotte   102

7.2   Drawing at five years, Charlotte   102

7.3   Drawings at eight years, Nicholas   104
7.4

7.5   Drawing at six years, the contemporary artist
      Michael Rothenstein (reproduced by courtesy of the
      Redstone Press)   105

7.6   Drawing at 10/11 years, 'M'   105

7.7   Drawing at six years, Henri de Toulouse-Lautrec
      (1864-1901)   107

7.8   Drawing at fourteen years, Nicholas   108

8.1   Seven-year old's copy of a portrait reproduction   117

8.2   Nine-year old's linocut reproductions of portraits   121

8.3   A nine-year old comparing with the original painting
      a postcard reproduction he has been studying in school   121

8.4   A seven-year old studies three portrait reproductions   123

8.5   A seven-year old's study of a Van Gogh self-portrait   126

8.6   Scott (aged seven) and his interpretation of the
      Gainsborough self-portrait   126

Preface

It is not usual for primary school teachers to have had specialist training in art, and it is thus perhaps not surprising that the subject is seldom as effective as it could be in the early years of schooling. This may seem to some readers to be a rather unfair claim: art is universally recognized as of importance in the curriculum of young children, they may argue, and one may see abundant evidence of this on entering any primary school. It is true that most, if not all, primary schools are adorned with children's drawings, paintings, models, and other artefacts. It is often a mistake, however, to suppose that these objects, visually attractive though many of them may be to adults, necessarily embody genuine experience in art. The manipulation of materials usually associated with art activity — paint, crayon, clay, paper — is not in itself any guarantee that the maker has undergone such experience (and, of course, this goes for adults as well as for children).

The very fact that working with art materials is an unquestioned part of the school life of any young child in Britain (and, indeed, throughout the western world), and that there seems to be general agreement that this is 'good', may in itself be a hazard. There is about the work of young children a natural charm, and there often seems to be no beneficial way in which a teacher can — or should — intervene. There seems to be little that can be positively *taught* without inhibiting — perhaps even permanently stifling — this attractive gaucheness, this directness, this supposed imaginative power. Art activity, it is implied, is *creative* activity; and creativity, being essentially personal, is something not to be interfered with. It is popularly supposed that artists are, by definition, creative individuals whose work depends upon a flow of original ideas; and, if such paragons are the model for art activity in schools, it is hardly surprising that many teachers feel at best ambivalent, at worst helpless, where their responsibility for the subject is concerned.

It is common to justify art in the education of young children on the grounds that, being essentially to do with the expression of feeling (loosely equated with creative experience), it complements the other, cognitive aspects of the curriculum. This book represents the view that such a separation is false. It represents a case for the *enmeshing* of knowledge and experience, the cognitive and the affective, in art; but, more than that, it represents a case for art as an illumination of the whole spectrum of a child's learning experiences.

★   ★   ★

Our chosen title, *Looking, Making, and Learning*, is intended to emphasize a fusion of aesthetic sensibility, discriminating control of materials, and rational planning. Over the last ten years or so, there has been an increasing tendency for this country's government to divide the school curriculum into the 'useful' and (in the best sense of the word) the 'useless' — to separate the 'hard' from the 'soft', science and technology from the arts and humanities. This kind of separation has a long history, and it has militated against art education. In 1835 the Government, alarmed (as now) at industrial competition from abroad, set up a House of Commons Select Committee on Arts and Manufactures. The Committee's Report led to the establishment of schools of design (with the aim of bolstering industry), distinct from the already-existing schools of 'fine art'. Sadly, the rift between art (seen as sharing with music, drama, and dance a responsibility in the school curriculum for developing 'aesthetic awareness') and design (which, in partnership with science and technology, is thought to be primarily of 'problem-solving' benefit) has deepened. This division not only of the scientific and technological from the artistic but also, within the field of art itself, a segregating of what has come to be called Craft, Design, and Technology from the 'aesthetic and creative' — and, furthermore, a stress upon the former — was indicated by the Secretary of State for Education when on 7 April 1987 he made the following pronouncement on the (then) proposed National Curriculum:

> We want to ensure that pupils have a well-balanced foundation curriculum ... which during the compulsory period includes not only maths and English, but also science, foreign languages, history, geography and technology in its various aspects. *Time should be found for music, art and physical education ...*
> (Department of Education and Science, 1982; my italic)

There is another division we wish to disclaim: that of theory and practice. This book is not a 'how-to-do-it'; it deals mainly with theoretical and philosophical issues. But, in doing so, it offers many practical examples — the classroom is seldom out of view. The good 'how-to-do-it' book is not to be despised; it can often provide a welcome life-line for the beginning teacher. Neither, though, may the acquiring of a theoretical grasp be deferred; in this, as in other fields, the practical and the theoretical go hand in hand.

So, in spite of their understandable craving for the expedient, ready-made art lesson, this book is offered to student teachers as well as to others more experienced. In it, we aspire to convey something of the extent and complexity of the field so often conveniently referred to as 'art' which, if it is to give children the richest possible learning opportunities, must range across the whole spectrum from art to design; deliberate and careful craftsmanship must become as valued as spontaneity and, to paraphrase the Gulbenkian Report (1982), appreciation must partner participation. Clearly, a subject embodying such a proliferation of experiences and demonstrating such obvious links with practically every other area of the curriculum may be seen to be of central importance. We therefore submit our book to all who administer or teach in primary schools, whether or not they have direct responsibility for art.

★   ★   ★

There is a kind of logic in the sequence of the contributions. In the first chapter Roy Prentice, for ten years Senior Art Adviser in East Sussex and currently Chairman of the Department of Art and Design at the Institute of Education, gives an account of significant publications and other initiatives in the twenty-two years since the appearance of the Plowden Report, *Children and their Primary Schools*. This is followed by a rather longer historical perspective, presented by Gillian Robinson, a former primary school teacher, now a lecturer at the Essex Institute of Higher Education. Next, Gillian Figg of the West Glamorgan Institute of Higher Education bases her proposal for a curriculum model on an analysis of the writings of a number of prominent art educators. These first three chapters may be taken as a setting of the scene.

Then, Vera Coghill (whose doctoral research, under the auspices of the Royal College of Art Design Education Unit, was founded on long experience of working with young children) and Ken Baynes (freelance teacher, designer, and member of the Design Council's Primary

Education Working Party) deal with play as a source of design activity; and Keith Gentle, an Inspector of Schools in Manchester, pursues the theme of play by focusing on the importance of children's direct sensory experience as a prerequistie for art activity.

Sheila Paine, a colleague in the Institute of Education, and long engaged in researching drawing development, follows with observations on an interesting though frequently overlooked aspect of children's drawing experience: humour.

And, lastly, my own chapter stresses the need, as I see it, for children's learning *about* art to be an integral part of their education in the subject.

We are all grateful to Denis Baylis, the Institute's Publications Officer, for much good advice, and for all his customary care and patience in helping to see this book through the press.

A.D.
April, 1989

References

Department of Education and Science (1987), *Secretary of State's National Curriculum Statement*, 7 April 1987. London: D E S.

Gulbenkian Report (1982), *The Arts in Schools*. London: Gulbenkian Foundation.

Chapter One
Some Recent Influences and Directions
Roy Prentice

Twenty years ago the publication of the Plowden Report *Children and Their Primary Schools* (1967), brought sharply into focus the desirability of direct experience, personal discovery and creative activity in the primary school curriculum. It heralded art as 'a form of communication and a means of expression of feelings which ought to permeate the whole curriculum and the whole life of the school'. Eleven years later, a survey by HM Inspectorate, *Primary Education in England* (Department of Education and Science, 1978a), revealed a depressingly different reality. In a majority of primary schools art was rarely seen to make a proper contribution to the development of children's perceptual skills through carefully considered programmes of work designed to encourage drawing, painting and modelling from direct observation. Art educators — particularly local education authority art advisers — expressed their mounting concern about the lack of art work derived from first-hand experience, together with the apparent relegation of art to a peripheral position in a large number of primary schools.

A welcome response from the Schools Council Art Committee, under the chairmanship of Ernest Goodman, was the publication of an Occasional Bulletin, *Art 7-11* (Schools Council Art Committee, 1978). Its purpose was to draw attention to serious concerns about art in the primary school curriculum and to provide some guidance and insight for class teachers and headteachers. Its warm reception in schools was due largely to its clear grasp of key issues and its straightforward, practical approach, which capitalized upon the sound experience of practising teachers. In addition the publication made accessible to a national audience of primary teachers the ideas of art advisers and the kind of work being undertaken by groups of teachers participating in INSET activities, particularly those initiated by Robert Clement in Devon and by Maurice Barrett in Redbridge. The importance of drawing was stressed in an attempt to overcome some common misconceptions and uncertainties which surround and often stifle children's development in drawing. Different functions of drawing — recording, analysis, communication and expression — were discussed in terms of learning and teaching.

At this time HM Inspectorate presented a view of 'good practice' in the publication *Art in Junior Education* (Department of Education and Science, 1978b), which contained descriptions of approaches to art teaching in nine schools. Elements which contribute to successful teaching and learning in art were identified. Attention was drawn to work of quality in a range of media derived from rich sensory experience which demonstrates the acquisition and refinement of skills alongside the development of a visual language.

Art in Junior Education referred to 'three major elements which stand out' in the schools under discussion: 'conviction', 'care' and 'expectation'. In each case teachers and headteachers displayed a strong commitment to art in the education of all children, and recognized its potential as a tool for learning. Concern was shown for the quality of the classroom environment and for the quality of interpersonal relationships — vital ingredients of a creative climate. The ideas and feelings of individuals were valued and tools and materials were handled with respect. High standards of work were expected and achieved through activities which were carefully planned, imaginatively presented, well resourced and progressively more demanding. Useful discussion points were intended to promote thought and action and encourage whole-staff discussion. A key question related to the appointment in each school of a consultant for art, a role which continues to be widely debated in terms of appropriate initial training and function.

In the mid-1970s the Schools Council rejected a proposal from the Art Advisers' Association for a three-year research project to investigate the function of drawing for children between eight and eleven years of age. However, a group of art advisers employed in the North Eastern Region mounted a large-scale touring exhibition called *Learning Through Drawing* (Art Advisers' Association, 1979). Their aim was to stimulate a wider interest in children's drawings and foster a deeper understanding of the educational potential of drawing. Included in this imaginatively presented and carefully documented exhibition were examples of different kinds of drawing by children and young people, from pre-school age to eighteen years of age. The exhibition was aimed at teachers and parents, and it was accompanied by a book of the same title which served as an informative catalogue (see p. 21, below.). It is encouraging that beyond the life of the exhibition many teachers continue to be influenced by this statement about drawing.

In it, drawing is presented as a process to be harnessed to promote learning, rather than a technique to be acquired: a process through which ideas and feelings can be communicated and expressed, in ways which embody meanings which could not adequately be conveyed through words and numbers. Furthermore, by highlighting the cross-curricular implications of a broad concept of drawing, the widely-held stereotype of drawing — what it should look like and the absence of talent which prevents 95 per cent of the population from engaging in it — is eroded.

With a desire to extend the ideas outlined in *Art 7-11*, the Schools Council Art Committee published a second Occasional Bulletin, *Resources for Visual Education 7-13* (Schools Council, 1981). It is significant that the title gives this publication a wider frame of reference, both in terms of the curriculum and of age range. It offers teachers an opportunity to consider in greater depth some of the material introduced in the previous publication, together with practical advice on the selection, organization and use of resources, within and beyond the school. Once again, case studies are used to advantage, in order to present the points under discussion in a realistic school context.

Teachers are encouraged to explore ways of working with children in museums and galleries, and it is heartening to note the marked increase in commitment to education which most museums and galleries have developed in recent years. Museum education departments and individual members of staff continue to explore ways in which links with schools can be strengthened. The recent national curriculum development project, Critical Studies in Art Education, 1981-1984, has done much to heighten awareness of the contribution that can be made by museums and galleries to the growth of children's understanding (Taylor, 1986).

* * *

In recent years there has been a proliferation of local education authority curriculum guidelines in all areas of the curriculum, in response to local and national directives. This has resulted in the production of many splendid guideline documents for art education which reflect the influences of the publications to which reference has already been made. Guidelines of this kind provide a sound basis for school-based INSET activities through which it is possible for headteachers and teachers — with advisory support — to begin to formulate whole-school policies for art. Publications of the calibre of *Some Functions of Art in the Primary School* (Rubens and Newland, 1983) enjoy a circulation far beyond the teachers for whom they were initially intended.

However, following the 1976 Ruskin College Speech by Prime Minister James Callaghan, those involved in, and concerned about, the arts in schools, were alarmed by the absence of well-informed comment on the arts in the vocationally-orientated national curriculum debate, which was rapidly gathering momentum. Under the chairmanship of Peter Brinson, then Director of the United Kingdom Branch of the Calouste Gulbenkian Foundation, an Advisory Committee was formed in the same year to consider the contribution to be made by the arts in the education of all children and young people. Four years later the Advisory Committee's Report, *The Arts in Schools*, was published by the Foundation (Gulbenkian Report, 1982). It is concerned with 'principles, practice and provision', and it is aimed at teachers, headteachers, administrators, governors, politicians and parents. Its purpose was to present a strong case for the arts to be put back on the mainstream agenda for the on-going curriculum debate.

The Report stresses that a curriculum in any art form should promote a dynamic relationship between two kinds of experience: 'participation' and 'appreciation'. Traditionally the visual arts in schools have been predominantly, if not exclusively, of a practical 'making and doing' nature. Certainly, at the primary stage children rarely, if ever, engaged in work of a critical or historical nature in art. Since the publication of the Report there has been a growing interest in critical and historical studies in art and design and there is evidence in a number of schools, including some primary schools, of curriculum innovation in this field. The work of artists, craftspeople and designers, from different cultures and different periods, offers a rich starting point for cross-curricular initiatives and a useful context within which a range of multicultural and gender issues can be addressed. The holistic nature of the primary curriculum facilitates experiential learning in art and design.

From the earliest years of schooling, the erosion of boundaries between school and the world beyond school can be aided by professional artists working closely with children and teachers. By placing an emphasis on the benefits to be gained from such collaboration, the Gulbenkian Report acknowledges the value of the Artists-in-Schools Scheme, administered by the regional arts associations, but even more opportunities for children to meet and work with a wide range of artists are recommended.

It is suggested that an appropriate curriculum in the visual arts for children between five and eleven years of age should enable them to:

(a) experiment with different media — watercolour, crayon, paper, cloth, clay, etc.;

(b) explore different techniques, tools and modes of manipulation in each — modelling, brush-work, etc.;

(c) understand the basic ideas of, for example, tone, colour, texture and contrast, and eventually more complicated ideas of, for example, balance, focus and proportion;

(d) begin to respond to a variety of styles and forms of visual art, including differences between cultural forms (e.g. Western, Oriental, African) and between historical periods (e.g. primitive, ancient, mediaeval, modern);

(e) develop an awareness of the use of visual symbols to convey ideas and feelings;

(f) develop an awarenes of design — the relationship between materials, forms and functions of objects and constructions;

(g) develop powers of observation and description. (ibid., p. 51)

Above all the Report reaffirms that in every school

where the arts flourish ... the headteacher and other staff appreciate and support them. In those schools where headteachers think the arts are marginal they suffer, whatever the economic circumstances. (ibid., p. 48)

In an increasingly severe educational and political climate, and during a period of economic constraint, the Gulbenkian Report helped to energize and focus the thinking of those involved in arts education. It made available to headteachers, administrators and politicians a philosophically-sound and logically-argued case for the arts to be taken seriously at all stages of education. Follow-up work undertaken by Kenneth Robinson (the Report's principle author) during the year following publication helped to further the influence of the Report, identify priorities and prepare the ground for further initiatives.

* * *

An opportunity to build upon the Gulbenkian Report's work presented itself with the establishment of the Schools Curriculum Development Committee as the main agency for curriculum development, following the Government's dissolution of the Schools Council. There was widespread support when it was announced that the first major curriculum project to be funded by S C D C was to be in the arts. In 1985 the Arts in Schools Project was launched, under the directorship of Kenneth Robinson, with funding in the region of £300,000 to cover the running costs of a central team for three years. Further support has since been provided by the Arts Council, the Crafts Council and the Gulbenkian Foundation.

The Project is founded on the belief that teacher development is necessary to achieve curriculum change. In each of the 18 participating local education authorities the work being undertaken is teacher-led. Teachers are involved in the process of change as members of local development groups, co-ordinated locally and nationally. The model is very different from that to which Schools Council projects had subscribed, which had relied heavily upon small central teams of 'experts' to produce materials to be used by teachers who had invested nothing in their development.

From an ambitious agenda three items seem worthy of special comment in the present context. Firstly, the involvement of both primary class teachers and secondary subject specialists allows the concept of a continuous education in art for all children to be fully explored within and between each phase of schooling. Secondly, the collaborative efforts of those responsible for the teaching of art, dance, drama, literature and music provide further insights into the similarities and differences between arts subjects, and the potential influence of the arts on other subjects. Thirdly, the continuing expansion of the role of professional artists in schools, as a result of closer working relationships between regional arts associations, visual arts and education officers and teachers. Over a short period of time significant advances have been made through the participation of artists in highly successful residencies and workshops in primary schools. Hitherto, the Artists-in-Schools Scheme had focused almost exclusively on secondary education. (The National Foundation for Educational Research is currently engaged in a two-year research project, 1987-1989, to evaluate the effectiveness of the work undertaken by artists in schools.)

*   *   *

The recent interest in and support for design education, fuelled by the intervention of central government and industry, has implications for the primary school curriculum. In 1984 the Design Council's Primary

Education Working Party was established, with the following terms of reference:

> To propose to the Design Council the policies and views that should be adopted with respect to design-related activities in primary schools and recommend the associated actions that should be taken by such organizations and individuals as may be appropriate. (Design Council, 1987, Introduction 1.1.)

The findings and recommendations are published in a report, *Design and Primary Education* (ibid.). The report emphasizes the importance of developing design-related activities throughout the primary curriculum. It strongly rejects the notion of a 'new subject', design, being introduced. Teachers are urged to find ways in which current approaches to teaching young children can provide opportunities for them to develop 'a capacity for design'. It is apparent that many areas of experience can offer such opportunities. Certainly there is an urgent need to articulate more precisely and exploit more fully the design element which is central to art and craft activities.

★   ★   ★

In spite of the efforts of those committed to the development of art in primary schools, and the accessibility of ideas on which good practice is based, the quality of art education in primary schools remains disappointingly uneven. Encouragement of 'self expression' and 'over directed' activities represent the two extremes of practice widely observed. In a large number of schools art continues to be reduced to a 'service role' for other subjects. There *are* schools where art is recognized as a powerful tool for learning and where children are helped to understand and respond to experience through sustained involvement in a range of progressively demanding art activities. Unfortunately, a desire for novelty too often leads to a frantic search for 'new ideas' and materials, resulting in children having a succession of superficial encounters with both. Commerical kits and colouring-books, 'how-to-do-it' publications and television programmes, help to perpetuate a prescriptive 'one-off', technique-dominated approach. In contrast, work of quality is to be found where sensitive teachers encourage, support and value each child's personal response to experience. As Ernest Goodman remarks in the foreword to *Resources for Visual Education 7-13*:

success in this field seems to depend more upon the degree of sensitivity, imagination and ingenuity of the teacher concerned than upon any personal skill in image-making — stimulating as this can be where it occurs and is wisely used. (Schools Council, 1981, p.5)

It is understandable that teachers who confess confusion about the purpose of art in primary education, and who themselves lack confidence when dealing with visual ideas and expressive media, should feel ill-equipped to structure and support children's learning in art. The appointment of properly-trained art consultants in primary schools — class teachers with particular responsibility for art in the curriculum — is an effective school-based means of improving this situation. Such consultants are able to offer colleagues confidence-inspiring support and guidance in the teaching of art; they are able to contribute the expertise required to formulate a policy for art education throughout a school and produce curriculum guidelines.

The National Society for Education in Art and Design has recognized the need for a single publication through which a wealth of authoritative material could be made accessible to all teachers. Through the efforts of the NSEAD the ideas and experience of a large number of teachers, teacher-trainers, HMI and LEA advisers were pooled, to provide the basis for the publication *Art, Craft and Design in the Primary School* (Lancaster, 1986). The intention was that this book should be used as a frame of reference for school-based discussion, practical INSET workshops and curriculum guideline documents. It is also heartening to see the NSEAD addressing primary teachers through the increasing number of scholarly articles with a primary focus included in the *Journal of Art and Design Education*.

*   *   *

In order to promote understanding and facilitate curriculum change in art throughout a school, it is necessary for an art consultant to function as a bridge between his or her colleagues and the wider field of theory and practice in art education. Only then will ideas of the order of those explored in the chapters which follow begin to influence classroom practice more widely. The concept of a consultant for each curriculum area (rather than a subject 'specialist') is supported by HM Inspectorate and reflected in the declared intentions of those responsible for courses of initial teacher education. However, in reality, a large number of BEd and PGCE courses currently fall far short of an adequate preparation of all students for the teaching of art (Cleave and Sharp, 1986). Sadly, at a time of expansion in primary teacher education nothing is being done to encourage highly qualified and imaginative art and design graduates to apply for specialist primary PGCE courses.

When considering the way forward for art in primary schools, a member of HM Inspectorate, with special responsibility for primary education, recently referred to the need for 'professional generosity'. In order to achieve a genuine understanding of the particularity of art experience within a holistic primary curriculum 'professional generosity' must, he argued, exist between art educators and primary specialists (together with LEA advisers, HMI and teacher educators). Only thus would a curriculum true to the development of children *and* true to the nature of art be created.

It is to achieve this end that most art educators have responded positively to the proposal to introduce a national curriculum, within which art is identified as a foundation subject. It is widely regarded as a rare opportunity to establish a broad-based structure to promote sequential learning in art for children between the ages of 5 and 16, informed by the considerable body of curriculum development undertaken in the field in recent years.

Such a development would encourage and support continuous learning in art within, and between, classes in a primary school, and between primary and secondary schools. It would make explicit that which is particular to learning in art, and identify ways in which art experiences can be used as rich starting points for cross-curricular explorations. Of particular importance is the need clearly to articulate the major role art has to play in the promotion of design activities across the curriculum.

At the level of initial primary teacher education the national curriculum debate facilitates reviews of BEd and PGCE course structures and content. Opportunities now exist for art and design components to have a more prominent position in courses of initial teacher education for all primary teachers.

It is for such reasons that there is an urgent need for art educators to consolidate their thinking and present a powerful case in support of programmes of study and attainment targets for art.

References
Art Advisers' Association (1979), *Learning Through Drawing*, a collaborative publication by North-Eastern Region members.

Central Advisory Council for Education (1967), *Children and Their Primary Schools*, The Plowden Report. London: HMSO.

Cleave, S. and Sharp, C. (1986), *The Arts: a preparation to teach*. Windsor: NFER-Nelson.

Department of Education and Science (1978a), *Primary Education in England: a survey by HM Inspectors of Schools*. London: HMSO.

———————— (1978b), *Art in Junior Education*. London: HMSO.

Design Council (1987), *Design and Primary Education*, a report of the Design Council's Primary Education Working Party. London: Design Council.

Gulbenkian Report (1982), *The Arts in Schools*. London: Gulbenkian Foundation.

Lancaster, J. (ed.) (1986), *Art, Craft and Design in the Primary School*. Corsham, Wilts.: National Society for Education in Art and Design.

Rubens, M. and Newland, M. (1983), *Some Functions of Art in the Primary School*. London: Inner London Education Authority Inspectorate.

Schools Council Art Committee (1978), *Art 7-11*. London: Schools Council.

Schools Council (1981), *Resources for Visual Education*, report from a curriculum development working group of the Schools Council Art Committee. London: Schools Council.

Taylor, R. (1986), *Educating for Art*. London: Longman.

Chapter Two

Stimulus for Art in the Primary School: an historical perspective
Gillian Robinson

A field without a memory of its past is in continual danger of rediscovering the wheel. (Eisner, 1972, p. 241)

This chapter is an investigation into the changing nature and role of stimulus for art in the primary school.

When art was officially acknowledged as being a desirable component of the curriculum in the 1830s and 1840s, it was because it was seen as a means of training potential designers and creating a design-conscious public. In 1835 the British Government had appointed a Select Committee to enquire into 'the best means of extending a knowledge of the arts and the principles of design among the people'. As a result, it was decided to include art teaching in the curriculum of state-aided schools. The art taught was consequently directly related to design and manufacture, and very formal. The children were set skill-orientated exercises. William Dyce's *Drawing Book of Elementary Examples in Outline* seems to have been influential from 1842 onwards (Sutton, 1967, p.94). The system involved the drawing and measuring of straight lines to begin with and progressed to the copying of geometrical figures (for illustration and a more detailed account the reader is referred to Littlejohns, 1928, pp.32-35). The outline of shapes such as acanthus leaves, which were considered beautiful and which had the further attraction of classical associations, were also copied. It was hoped, says Dick Field, that 'in copying the outlines of beautiful shapes the child would imbibe the principles of beauty' (Field, 1970, p.6).

Stuart Macdonald (1970, p.153) describes the children in schools at the time as working mostly on slates with slate pencils from sets of diagrams which teachers could buy and, as Sutton (1967, p.54) informs us that the plates from William Dyce's drawing book were issued as separate sheets, it is likely that these are what they were copying. Sometimes the children even worked with chalk on desks painted black or on a black strip a foot deep painted round the room.

In 1852 Henry Cole, a pioneer of state art education, in an address given at the opening of a new elementary school in Westminster, proclaimed a national system of art education in the public day schools. In practice it did not differ much from Dyce's system. The primary and first grade course was strictly utilitarian and had accuracy as its main objective: the children began with linear geometry and perspective and progressed to outlines of simple objects, copying from flat exemplars like diagrams. The course progressed with the copying of three-dimensional forms, the flat copy of the outline of the human figure and animals, and culminated in the copying and painting of flowers.

In the back of a copy of a first grade drawing book, produced in the Royal Schools Series (six books priced at 2d each, sadly undated), is detailed a systematic drawing course offering stimulus material from Royal Drawing Cards for Slate Work through to Royal First Grade Test Papers and progressing from examples of 'straight lines' to 'floral design and vases'. It represents a very thorough but totally inflexible course. Very specific instructions are issued to the teacher. For example, he is told that the pupil has three very 'interesting' things to do:

> First, he has to imitate the form, to reproduce, line by line, each straight line in the example with perfect straightness, each curved line with a curve in the same character, and faithfully copied from start to finish; secondly he has to do this with a firm free line ... thirdly, he has to keep the paper clean.

The system still allowed for no imagination or freedom and was in line with the belief that the child was there as a receptacle for knowledge. (For a further account of the copying methods used at this time the reader should consult Tomlinson, 1944, pp.8-10.)

The Log Book of a school in Essex dating from December 1902 shows the criteria to be those of neatness and accuracy: we learn from one entry that 'The drawing of the boys is accurate and neat and generally well done'. 'Drawing from objects' was added in September 1905, still only for the boys, and, in April 1906, freehand and ruler work. We may take this as being fairly representative of the general approach to such work in schools at this date.

Professor Louis Arnaud Reid, a school pupil at about the same time, remembered his own childhood experience of 'art lessons' as follows:

The 'art lesson' consisted of exercises such as learning to draw perfectly straight lines of exact length, or the symmetrical curves of a vase, or flower pots or buckets and mops or doorplates. 'Expression', nowadays taken for granted, was unheard of, at least in ordinary schools. (Reid, 1961, p.271)

In this period of formalism the children had to learn techniques before they could 'do art'. An amusing, though sobering, example of this attitude persisting in some schools in the 1940s was described to the writer by Pamela Diamand, the daughter of Roger Fry — painter and art critic — as she talked about her recollection of art teaching just before the end of the war when her own son Roger was at primary school in Essex:

they were given a milk bottle at the other end of the room, for an hour or something, to draw and of course what could these poor kids do? So he started drawing war in the air, you know fights, air fights between the aeroplanes. Of course the others came to see and there was a slight commotion and he got caned. (Diamand, in conversation, 17 April, 1984)

Although not evidenced by the school just cited, the attitude to children's art had been changing imperceptibly since as far back as 1878, when Ebenezer Cooke read before the Education Society a paper illustrated by children's drawings. It is recorded in his obituary in the *Journal of Education* (1914, .p.115) as being 'the earliest attempt to investigate this branch of psychology', and the precursor of James Sully's studies. In 1895 Sully was to publish *Studies of Childhood*, in which there are two chapters on the art of children, entitled 'The Child as Artist' (ch. IX) and 'The Young Draughtsman' (ch. X). In them Sully frequently refers to the work of Cooke. He also spoke for the first time of 'child art' when he referred to the art of children being a thing by itself (ibid., p.385).

Another of Cooke's papers, read in 1884 and entitled 'Our Art Teaching and Child Nature' (*Journal of Education*, 1 December, 1885, and 1 January, 1886), was also influential. In it he mentions the work of T.R. Ablett, who was concerned about the standard of art teaching. He indicates Ablett's emphasis on observing the child, quoting him as saying: 'Is our system adapted to our pupils? ... Let not the aim of technical skill stagnate the intellect. Do not copy merely, but originate, invent, educate ...' He goes on: '[Ablett] felt and suggested that early art, the child's ways, and nature were related and would assist each other.'

In 1888 Ablett founded the Royal Drawing School, which held its first exhibition of children's work in 1890. He advocated that the real aim of child art was 'drawing for delight'. Carline feels that Ablett was at one with Cooke in:

> stressing the educational value of learning to draw and in rejecting the long-established respect for neatness and precision in outline as the main criteria of merit in children's work and [in recognizing] instead, its force and vitality. (Carline, 1968, p.5)

Following on from the questioning of the value of academic drawing, there came a growing interest in the training of the visual memory.

Memory Drawing
Ablett was interested in this approach, and included 'snap-shot' drawing in the Royal School of Drawing syllabus (Carline, 1968, p.133). The use of memory in the training of the artist was, however, traditional. The belief in the value of the training of the memory in art seems in more recent times to have originated with Lecoq de Boisbaudran, and was set out in his book/*Training of the Memory in Art*, published in 1897. He emphasized the aspect of stored observation, whereas Catterson Smith (of the Birmingham School of Art) did not think it important to learn visual forms by heart. He agreed with Lecoq, however, concerning the relationship of the memory to the imagination. Catterson Smith's students viewed lantern slides of animals and had then to draw them from memory as if from another viewpoint. His method, known as 'shut-eye drawing', was a way of impressing the form of the object on the children's minds. The procedure, described by Sutton (1967, p.267), was as follows: the children, with outstretched finger, traced in the air the shape of the object; then, after repeating the process with the eyes shut, they looked again. A series of drawings was then made; the first with the eyes shut, the second from memory with the eyes open, and the third from the object.

But was it an effective way of stimulating art activity? Laura Plaisted obviously thought so, for she explained the value of memory drawing as follows:

> Drawing from memory trains the child to recall memory images, to discover discrepancies, and to create a desire to make good such discrepancies as [the] occasion arises. It should have a large place in any scheme. (Plaisted, 1925, p.118)

and

> steady practice in drawing from memory objects simple enough to stimulate
> the child to do his best work will prove an excellent means of teaching him to
> 'see' and of developing and revealing to him his own powers of graphic
> representation. (ibid.)

She also offers advice on how to create a situation in which memory
drawing can occur, suggesting that the very presence of work on the
walls, or a 'model placed in a prominent position in the room', will often
promote memory drawing 'since after the first observation the young
child seldom turns around to look at the model until he has completed
his drawing'. Whether or not this is the case is a matter for debate, as
Freeman and Janikoun demonstrated in their research (1972). She also
advocates regular exercises in drawing from memory, which should
include 'the sketching of simple objects in daily life before they are
attempted from a model, as well as those which have been drawn in the
previous lesson'. Alternatively the work could consist of 'a series of
attempts during which the model is alternately exposed and hidden
from view'. She offers a further suggestion that work may be introduced
by announcing the subject the day before, allowing for an opportunity
to prepare out of school.

A memory image which allows for more in terms of imagination is
mentioned by Roger Fry in the first of a series of five lectures given in
the 1920s and entitled 'Principles of Design'.* Fry writes:

> A piece of paper is not to a child a surface to be made interesting to the eye,
> although children have a strong feeling for the sensual pleasures of the eye —
> but it is a means to the firmer possession of the memory images of desirable
> and interesting things which fill his mind.

Fry felt, however, that in spite of the intensity of a child's reactions to an
object or event, the memory images which a child has are nevertheless
'vague, fleeting and elusive things'. However, the reason a child begins
to make a picture, according to Fry, stems from this very fact of 'vague
elusiveness, for he wishes to possess the memory image in a more
definite and precise form'. The child's drawings are seen as a means to
this end, that is, achievement of a form which will satisfy him in both
detail and precision.

* The lectures are unpublished and are among the Fry papers, King's
College, Cambridge (FP 10/c/1).

Helga Eng, writing in 1931, also made the observation, when studying the drawings of her niece, that the mental pictures of children are 'blurred and incomplete' (p.129). She nonetheless felt that a child draws 'by making use of its mental pictures of objects'. She believed that the free drawing of children before school is almost entirely from memory. She says: 'Children do not look at the things which they represent but draw them out of their heads' (Eng, 1931, p.124), and she gives as the chief reason a child draws from memory that children's drawing is 'ideomotive' both in origin and in its early development. The child repeats lines and forms so many times that he is able to produce them on paper 'almost mechanically'. Fry found that sometimes when a child finds a new symbol which satisfies him as a representation of an object which he likes 'he feels such satisfaction in it that he goes on repeating it mechanically to multiply ... his means of possession'.

Karl Buhler (quoted in Viola, 1944, pp.13-14) felt that it is a slightly more complex process, stating that what a child works from is not just memory images but 'memory arrangements of judgements'. In other words, as well as visual sensations, the child's personality, needs, feelings and experience also affect the images which are stored (Eng, 1931, p.135). Hanson also explains that:

> Seeing is an experience, a retinal reaction is only a physical state — a photochemical excitation ... People, not their eyes, see. (Hanson, 1984, p.71)

Working from memory, 'as does a child', was part of the method of Alberto Giacometti, the sculptor and painter. In *Giacometti: sculptures, paintings, drawings,* he writes:

> For me, working from memory is just a matter of trying when I'm alone to remake things I've seen. Because in working from life, one always sees much more than one can cope with. In working from memory one tries to retain what has struck one most forcibly. (Giacometti, 1981, pp.10, 11)

The *Handbook of Suggestions for Teachers* (published from 1938 onwards), recommended that the visual memory should be trained, and it was still a feature of art education until the 1940s; but the Ministry of Education's 1946 publication made no mention of memory drawing, emphasizing freedom for the child. So what took its place? We find that methods developed almost imperceptibly from memory drawing of an object recently observed to memory drawing from observed situations combined with an element of imagination. This brings us to the third section of this chapter, which will deal with the inner vision of the child, or that of the child and the teacher together, as a stimulus for picture-making.

Self expression

At the beginning of the twentieth century circumstances were more favourable than previously (when the ideas of Ablett and Cooke seemed ahead of their time and were therefore scarcely taken notice of) for new ideas about child art to be accepted and flourish. Research was being carried out into the psychology of early childhood. Wilhelm Viola (1944, pp.13, 14) mentions the work of S. Levinstein (1904), William Sterm (who wrote on the development of early childhood up to the sixth year of age) and Karl Bhuler (1919, who wrote on the mental development of the child, and whose attitude was based on the theories of Sully, Levinstein and Kirchensteiner). Also, in 1910, Roger Fry held his first Post-Impressionist exhibition, which included the work of Henri Rousseau (1844-1910), the French 'primitive' painter. The whole connection between child art and the art of the untrained primitive, and the consequent question of whether training in art is necessary, was once again raised. Macdonald (1970) suggests that the prevailing psychological theories, together with the increased awareness of the aesthetic merits of primitive art and the developing appreciation of the characteristics of modern art, were some of the factors contributing to the growing recognition of child art.

Fry, who had observed the spontaneous drawing of his own daughter, Pamela, and the children of other artists, decided to hold an exhibition of children's paintings in his newly-opened Omega workshop in Fitzroy Square. To this exhibition came Marion Richardson. She discovered that her thoughts about art education were in line with Fry's expressed contempt for the way drawing was taught in schools.

In a letter to his daughter dated 17 March, 1917, which she read to me, Fry describes the pictures which the pupils of Marion Richardson had done as 'simply too lovely for anything'. He goes on to describe his determination to show them to the Minister of Education to 'see if we can't do something to stop the teaching of art'. At the end of the letter he remarks: 'I dare say they'd never come to being artists, but the imagination is astonishing. I long to show them to you.' What did Marion Richardson use as a stimulus for her pupils to work from? How did she achieve these results? Did they work from memory? She had been a pupil of Catterson Smith and had worked with methods similar

to those of Lecoq de Boisbaudran. Catterson Smith had used lantern
slides when he trained his pupils to draw from memory, but Marion
Richardson had no such pictures to show her children. She decided to
describe to them vividly everyday events and scenes, hoping to produce
in the children's imagination 'mind pictures'. It was from these 'mind
pictures' that the children worked. Pamela Diamand gave an account of
her methods as follows:

> She would describe what she had decided was to be the picture ... She went to
> the Russian Ballet and she decided to describe that to them and they did some
> very charming things from that. (in conversation, 17 April, 1984)

and she also made them illustrate things that they actually saw. Mrs.
Diamand remembered one scene of 'market on Saturday night. There
were the flowers and apples and oranges that were sold in the market'
(ibid.).

Marion Richardson gave lectures using slides of the children's work;
teachers fell in love with the drawings because they were so 'natural and
spontaneous'. She says:

> I knew many of the teachers decided there and then that, given permission,
> they would gladly abandon the formal syllabus of work which hitherto had
> guided them and trust to the children's natural interest as the mainspring of
> their art teaching. (Richardson, 1948, p.75)

Marion Richardson was appointed to the London Inspectorate in 1930.
Readers particularly interested in her work and the impact which she
made on the art teaching world should consult the special number of
Athene (Ellis, 1947), which was published in commemoration of her, or
her own writing, *Art and the Child*, first printed in 1948 following her
death in 1946.

But was this freedom of expression entirely a good thing? Were there
not inherent dangers in moving away from a set syllabus and direct
methods of teaching? Opinions differed. Marion Richardson's methods
were certainly approved of by Roger Fry who, in the preface to the
catalogue of the exhibition of the work of her pupils (Omega
Workshop, Fitzroy Square, February 1919), wrote disparagingly of the
direct methods of teaching as preventing children from 'producing
anything of the slightest value when they are young' and doing 'nothing
to enable them to express themselves when they grow up'. He
continued:

the average child has extraordinary inventiveness in design and the average
adult has none whatever ... and in between these two states occurs the process
known as art teaching. (Fry, 1919)

He therefore applauded the approach of Marion Richardson, who
refused to give direct instruction. She recognized children's need to
express their ideas and feelings in their own way.

Others, however, could not give her methods their wholehearted
approval. Louis Arnaud Reid (1964, p.271) comments that as
expressiveness caught on many teachers became obsessed with the fear
of imposing anything, and Rudolf Arnheim identifies the difficulties
which could arise. He writes:

the modern methods have given an outlet to the aspects of the child's mind
that were crippled by the traditional procedure of copying models with a
sharpened pencil. But there is an equal danger in preventing the child from
using pictorial work for clarifying his observation of reality and for learning
to concentrate and to create order. (quoted in Sutton, 1967, p.281)

The artist Victor Pasmore, one of the chief advocates of the spirit of
the Bauhaus, comments that in the new art teaching the fact that the
child is not required to imitate the adult means that the child's own
limitations are an acceptable part of the work. The process of teaching
therefore becomes focused not on correcting a likeness to an example
but on the encouragement of natural development. Given the stimulus
and the materials, the child will teach himself through his own activity.
As Carline says, 'Sensibility was the essential quality to be encouraged:
technical competence was of minor consideration' (1968, p.171).

Some scathingly described it as having precipitated what came to be
known as the 'slosh era', which continued long after Marion
Richardson's death. Says Clifford Ellis:

So now, 20 years later, we have the dogmas of, 'The New Art', of 'Slosh'
(with invariably big brushes), of standardized opaque powder colour, and, in
short, a set of narrow 'academic' rules as tight as any of the conventions
Marion Richardson opposed. (Ellis, 1947, p.21)

Associated with the approach in the 1930s was the idea of the 'child as
artist'. A book written by Evelyn Gibbs in 1934 has as the first chapter
'The "artist" in children' and R.R. Tomlinson's book of 1944 has as its
title *Children as Artists*. Rhoda Kellogg — a nursery school educator

since 1928, with a collection of half a million drawings — wrote in *Analyzing Children's Art:*

> In terms of spontaneous art, every child is a 'born artist' who should be allowed to scribble without oppressive guidance in 'art education'. (Kellogg, 1969, p.266)

The 'child art revolution', as it came to be known, spans at least forty years, with its core of activity placed around 1930-1960. Dick Field observes:

> In the revolution in attitudes towards children which occurred at about the turn of the century, art education had a part to play; and from that time on for almost a half century, art education could claim to be progressive and in the forefront of educational development, and the scope it gave for creative activity. But the focus of interest and need has shifted elsewhere: society has demanded more of science, mathematics and language; and the imagination of educationists has moved to the improvement of teaching processes in these areas. (Field, 1970, p.72)

Art also moved consequently into the service of other areas of the curriculum and was possibly one of the reasons why drawing with a magnifying glass in one hand became so prevalent a form of art education — the 'learning through drawing' approach, rather than learning *about* drawing or learning *about* art or artists' work.

Observational drawing
Observational drawing as a method can be traced back to the syllabus in state-aided schools as a later development of the freehand copy and the linear drawings of the acanthus leaf:

> What is known as mass drawing, done with a stump, light and shade, 'chiaroscuro', came into fashion. Later still came the 'back to nature' cult which introduced the drawing of natural forms such as plants, flowers and fruit, and fashioned objects, flower-pots, jam jars, boots, chairs — in fact still life. (Tomlinson, 1966, pp.12-13)

There was no mention of imagination. They were dull still-life objects, to which the French, *nature morte*, seems very appropriately applied. The examination system was partly the cause. Marion Richardson tried to overcome the difficulty by using dramatic lighting effects.

So how does this relate to the situation in more recent times? Observational drawing as a stimulus for art proliferated in the 1970s as 'a form of enquiry', a 'means of awareness' and a 'fostering of inquisitiveness' (Field, 1970, p.63), and it is still very much with us. If the casual observer walked into one of the more recently-built open-plan schools it would seem as though things had turned full circle. There are the twigs and flowers; children drawing a bleached sheep's skull or an old plough. Is this the teaching of skills and representational drawing all over again? Has the influence of Marion Richardson and 'free expression' so soon been forgotten? The objects are there to stimulate the children's vision and feed the imagination, based on a firm belief in first-hand experience which offers an opportunity to investigate and respond to what is in front of them and is an advance on the 'teaching of skills'.

First-hand experience

How far is first-hand experience a valuable stimulus for art? In *Learning Through Drawing* (Art Advisers' Association, 1979), a booklet published to accompany an exhibition of drawings by children, mounted by the North Eastern Region of the Art Advisers' Association, there is printed the following observation:

> During the period between eight and puberty, many children embark on a quest which is never fully resolved throughout their lives, that of how to accommodate the difference between the apparent facts of Reality and Imagination through their response to revealed and observed experience.

If we accept that art is a form of knowing and that one of its functions is to enable children to understand and organize their world, then perhaps first-hand experience is the most appropriate stimulus for art in the primary school. Reid suggests that there is a sense in which all knowledge really assimilated must be assimilated through active acquaintance (1961, p.34). A Schools Council Occasional Bulletin (1981, p.7; see also pp.3 and 7 above) also advocates the use of first-hand experience as a stimulus. In the introduction it is claimed that a common factor among teachers who are able to encourage their children to develop work of a consistently high quality is their conviction that first-hand experience is at the root of their achievement. Maurice Rubens, in the introduction to the booklet, *Some Functions of Art in the Primary School* (written in collaboration with Mary

Newland), states that its intention is to 'suggest approaches to visual education which emphasise a personal response to direct experience'. He goes on to say that drawing is a practical starting point for learning to look:

> The pencil's purpose is not to 'Teach Drawing', its purpose is to hold the child longer in the presence [of the object he is appraising], to prolong the period of attentive looking. (Rubens and Newland, 1983, p.12)

But does focused attention necessarily result in a personal response? The danger is that the broader concept of first-hand experience narrows down in practice to become just the experience of observational drawing and the focus of attention imperceptibly becomes the minutiae of the specimen. What began, perhaps, as an art-based activity becomes a scientific investigation — art with a microscope (Fig. 2.1).

Field sees the danger that 'if the child is constantly given the real thing to look at and told to observe and record all the detail [he or she] will be left with the feeling that all art is about accurate recording'. He says that at the right time the reference to nature is surely valid but blames such incidents as the child being taken to the window to be shown that the sky is not just a blue strip at the top of the page but 'comes right down to the ground' for some children's failure to realize that 'art is not merely

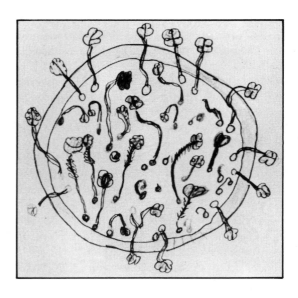

**Figure 2.1:
Seven-year old's
drawing from direct
observation, with
the aid of a
magnifying glass.**

imitation but speaks in a language of its own' (Field and Newick, 1973, p.144). The writer maintains that first-hand experience and observational drawing are valuable in aiding perceptual development. The Schools Council (1978; see p.1, above) suggests also that it provides children with a 'reservoir of images', thus nurturing the visual imagination. All children in the primary school can benefit from a rich collection of source material to see, to touch and to handle, and which can provide inspiration for drawing:

> There is an infinite delight in small things, to be seen, smelled, listened to, touched, felt for their texture or smoothness, or cool or warmth ... the aesthetic pleasure is direct ... the things speak for themselves. (L.A. Reid in Ross, 1982, p.24)

But there are aspects of first-hand experience other than observational drawing which are, though not often exploited, valuable stimuli for art in the primary school: for example, dance and movement, or watching an artist at work. The teacher should beware lest observational drawing, as an end in itself, become a straitjacket for art in the school. For one must enquire whether visual education is a satisfactory replacement for art education. The two cannot be synonymous, for observational drawing, valuable though it is, suggests accuracy of measurement, conformity to a copied image, and the expectation that the child will observe detail carefully and create an image which is as near to the original as possible. Its value lies in its encouragement of concentration and sensitivity to the subtleties of colour and form. Nevertheless the question has to be asked: 'Is it stimulus for art or is it rather art being a stimulus for learning about something else?'

Other areas of the curriculum
Although art is often used in the primary school in the service of other subjects, there are neglected opportunities for stimulus for *art* from other areas. In addition to movement and dance, which have already been mentioned, music and topic work are prime examples. In a topic on farms, a class of six-to-eight year olds discussed a poem about a lonely scarecrow. Some of the children then painted this scarecrow as they imagined it to be. One or two of the paintings convey this feeling of loneliness, especially that shown in Fig. 2.2, which was painted by a child who found observational drawing difficult.

Figure 2.2: Seven-year old's painting, enriched with crayon

Music can also be used as stimulus for art. Research into this area is currently being carried out by Alexandra Fairman, on the relationship between sounds and the elements of abstract works of art. Some of her work has taken place in primary schools. With a class of nine-year olds the writer used the stimulus of two contrasting electronic sequences of sound on tape. The drawings which resulted can be seen in Figs. 2.3 and 2.4. Interesting suggestions for collaboration between the arts can be found in a book written in 1976 by Arden Rose, *Interacting Through Creative Arts Activities.*

Some stimulus is not planned but arises from other activities. It is valuable if the teacher can recognize these situations and utilize them. One such occasion was when some very exciting work in art arose from the imaginative writing of an eight-year-old boy in the writer's own class. Robert was invited to write a story about anything which really interested him. He wrote this story over a period of three days. During the writing of it he was completely engrossed. The tiny figures which illustrate his story were so reminiscent of Joan Miro's lithographs that Robert was asked if he had heard of the artist (Fig. 2.5). He had not, but when he was shown Miro's work he became very excited by it and

Figures 2.3 and 2.4: Nine-year old children's drawings in response to electronic sound sequences

produced more of his own figures on a large scale, each having a Miro-like quality (Fig. 2.6).

This surprise element, the allowing for the unexpected, is, in the opinion of the writer, one of the most important aspects of stimulus in the primary school because it allows for personal, and therefore relevant, response from the child.

Robert's response to the work of an artist brings us to the consideration of artists' work as a stimulus for art-making activities.

Artists' work

Perhaps the most neglected of all is the stimulus which can be derived from an awareness of our heritage in art. The idea of art itself as an aid to developing children's art in the primary school encompasses three facets which sometimes overlap:

(a) the teaching of art history;
(b) encounters with real works of art; and
(c) contact with artists.

Figure 2.5: Illustration by Robert, aged 8, to his own story

The report *The Arts in Schools* (see p.4, above), published by the Calouste Gulbenkian Foundation in 1982, states:

> Meeting and working with living artists can give children valuable insight into the nature of these processes and into the interests and motivations which drive them. (Gulbenkian Report, 1982, p.117, para.193)

and in the Schools Council Working Paper No. 54, Malcolm Ross observes that:

> Contact with the contemporary arts, or with the living world of the art of the past, would seem to be an indispensable source of personal stimulus and nourishment. (Ross, 1975, p.44)

Some current research in art education is concerned with works of art as a stimulus, involving children's perception of artists' work, and practical work stemming from children's acquaintance with pictures in galleries and artists in residence. Anthony Dyson (1982, pp.123-133; and pp.110-130, below) is among those concerned with teaching the

Figure 2.6: Robert's drawing (right) compared with one by Joan Miro

history of art in the primary school and is involved in research in this area. His paper 'Art History in Schools' puts forward a strategy for the teaching of art history in general education. The current research work of Alfred Harris and others, 'Resources for Art Eduction', begun in 1981 in the Department of Art and Design at the Institute of Education, University of London, is concerned with overcoming the limited and prescribed ways of working which teachers often adopt, by working with the recorded ideas of artists. The conflict which often arises between these ideas offers the children something to consider, encouraging them to be involved in open discussion and to feel free to indicate preferences.

Examples of encounters with works of art and meetings with real artists are recorded in papers or reports of experiments. A report by Helen Luckett, published by the Arts Council, *Through Children's Eyes: a fresh Look at contemporary art* (1982), concerns an exhibition organized at Southampton Art Gallery. This exhibition of contemporary work was visited and investigated over the course of several months during 1981-82 by two classes of seven- and eight-year olds. The description of the children's reactions to the fourteen modern works of art is inspiring. Obviously much time and effort had gone into preparing the children so that they could respond as fully as possible to the objects in the gallery. The effect of the children's experience of such a rich stimulus permeated the rest of their work so that 'it was almost possible to see their imaginations extend and develop and to see their concept of the world grow larger'. The teachers involved, however, felt that most importantly the children 'learnt the ability to see creatively'.

The Arts Council is also involved in sponsoring projects through its 'Artists in Schools' scheme. There are two ways in which children can come into contact with 'real artists' and be given the opportunity to discuss their work and ideas. Either artists spend two to eight days in school or children spend time in a gallery which has an artist in residence.

Another instance of children having direct contact with an artist is reported by Julia Hagedorn in *Junior Education* (1982). Artist Jon George is an abstract painter and a member of Art Place Trust, which is a group of artists, dancers and sculptors who are in the process of converting a factory site at Tower Hamlets, London, into studios and an arts centre. He visited the children in their school for two weeks and encouraged them in their own painting. Then, as a culmination of this, the children visited him in his studio. This reciprocal interest is important. Not only do children benefit from the stimulus of observing a real artist at work, but for some artists the ideas and work of the children could be of real value.

In 1980-81 the Arts Council organized at London's Whitechapel Art Gallery an exhibition of the Leicestershire collection of works of art for use by schools and colleges. The collection concentrates on the works of younger artists whilst also acquiring limited edition prints by better-known painters and sculptors. Andrew Fairbairn, in the introduction to the catalogue, defends the collection of original works of art in schools as an 'indispensable ingredient' (Fairbairn, 1980, p.7)

Critical Studies in Art Education is a project (1981-1984), directed by Rod Taylor and based at the Drumcroon Education Art Centre, in Wigan. It aims to 'complement the essentially expressive nature of art teaching by developing the more reflective and contemplative aspects of the subject' and to 'develop and extend pupils' opportunities of studying original works of art and craft'. The related occasional publications which the teacher should consult are No. 1., *Broadening the Context* and No. 2., *The Illuminating Experience*, published by the Schools Council in 1982, and the culminating publication (1986), *Educating for Art.*

Conclusion

This chapter has looked at stimulus for art in the primary school in an historical framework whilst also raising certain questions about its nature and its value. Although, in the words of Field, 'in the normal process of change and development we must give a new orientation to art education' (1970, p.128), we must not be too dismissive of previous attitudes to stimulus for art activities or too hasty in jumping on current bandwagons. Children benefit from a heterogeneity of stimuli: minute and detailed observation, first-hand experience (including kinaesthetic stimulus), stimulus from other subjects in the curriculum and, perhaps above all, an awareness of the work of other artists. A little girl in my class became really excited by a book on the paintings of Van Gogh, which I took into the classroom. She spent a long time looking at the pictures and finally asked if she could paint one of them (Fig. 2.7) At the end of the day she had produced a living and brightly-coloured picture based on Van Gogh's last painting, 'Crows in the Wheatfields', 1890. The way she had approached it seemed to indicate that it was both the colour and the brush strokes which attracted her to Van Gogh's work and stimulated her to try and emulate him. At the end of the day she wrote triumphantly: 'I tried to be an artist'.

Figure 2.7: Nine-year old girl's picture, painted after studying Van Gogh's 'Crows in the Wheatfields' (1890)

References

Art Advisers' Association (1979), *Learning Through Drawing*, a collaborative publication by North-Eastern Region members.

Carline, R. (1968), *Draw They Must*. London: Arnold.

Department of Education and Science (1978), *Primary Education in England: a survey by HM Inspectors of Schools*. London: HMSO.

Dyson, A. (1982), 'Art history in schools: a comprehensive strategy', *Journal of Art and Design Education*, Vol.1, No.1.

Eisner, E. (1972), *Educating Artistic Vision*. London: Macmillan.

Ellis, C. (1947), 'Marion Richardson, 1892-1946', *Athene*, special number (Society of Education Through Art), Vol.4, No.1.

Eng, H. (1931), *The Psychology of Children's Drawings*. London Routledge, 1970 ed.

Fairbairn, A. (1980), *The Leicestershire Schools's Art Collection*, catalogue. London: Arts Council of Great Britain.

Field, D. (1970), *Change in Art Education*. London: Routledge.

Freeman, N.H. and Jakinou, R. (1972), 'Intellectual realism in children's drawing of a familiar object with distinctive features', *Child Development*, Vol.43, pp.1116-1121.

Fry, R. (1919), *The Work of the Pupils of Miss M. Richardson*, catalogue. London: Omega Workshop.

Giacometti, A. (1981), *Sculptures, Paintings and Drawings*, catalogue. London: Arts Council of Great Britain.

Gulbenkian Report (1982), *The Arts in Schools*. London: Gulbenkian Foundation.

Hagedorn, J. (1982), 'Through the eyes of an abstract painter', *Junior Education*, Vol.16, No.11, November.

Hanson, N.R. (1984), Observation' in C. Harrison and F. Orton (eds.), *Modernism, Criticism, Realism*. London: Harper & Row.

Kellogg, R. (1969), *Analysing Children's Art*. California: Mayfield.

Lecoq de Boisbaudran, H. (1897), *Training of the Memory in Art*. London: Macmillan, 1911 ed.

Littlejohns, J.(1928), *Art in Schools*. London: University of London Press.

Luckett, H. (1982), *Through Children's Eyes: a fresh look at contemporary art*. London: Arts Council of Great Britain.

Macdonald, S. (1970), *The History and Philosophy of Art Education*. London: University of London Press.

Ministry of Education (1938-1946), *A Handbook of Suggestions for Teachers*. London: HMSO.

Plaisted, L. (1925), *Handwork in Early Education*. Oxford:

Reid, L.A. (1961), *Philosophy and Education*. London: Heinemann, 1966 ed.

Richardson, M. (1948), *Art and the Child*. London: University of London Press.

Rose, A. (1976), *Interacting Through Creative Arts Activities*. California: Learning Handbooks.

Ross, M. (1975), *Arts and the Adolescent*, Schools Council Working Paper 54. London: Evans/Methuen Educational.

Ross, M. (ed.) (1982), *Curriculum Issues in Arts Education*, Vol.1, The Arts and Personal Growth; Vol.2, The Aesthetic Imperative; Vol.3, The Development of Aesthetic Experience. Oxford: Pergamon.

Rubens, M. and Newland, M. (1983), *Some Functions of Art in the Primary School*. London: Inner London Education Authority.

Sully J. (1895), *Studies of Childhood*. London: Longman.

Sutton, G. (1967), *Artisan or Artist?* Oxford: Pergamon.

Taylor, R. (1982), Schools Council Reports, No.1, *Broadening the Context*; No.2, *The Illuminating Experience*. London: Schools Council.

——————— (1986), *Educating for Art*. London: Longman.

Tomlinson, R.R. (1944), *Children as Artists*. Harmondsworth: King Penguin.

——————— (1966), *The Growth of Child Art*. London: University of London Press.

Viola, W. (1944), *Child Art*. London: University of London Press.

Chapter Three
Towards a Curriculum Model For Primary Art, Craft and Design
Gillian Figg

Not all teachers need a curriculum model in order to operate effectively in the primary classroom: there are those 'intuitive' teachers who epitomize all that is traditionally considered to be good primary art practice. However, there are others, amongst whom I number myself, who, for various reasons, feel they need a model or 'map' to help them rationalize what they do. Indeed, in the present educational climate, with an increasing call for accountability in all areas of the curriculum, for teachers to be able to justify their practice with confidence can only strengthen the place of art, craft and design in the primary school.

In this chapter I shall give an account of my own search for an appropriate curriculum model. I shall begin by reviewing what already exists in the literature and synthesize what seems to be most relevant from my own point of view as a teacher. I shall then go on to show how I use this theoretical framework in order to arrive at specific curriculum content.

My purpose in writing this is to demonstrate how the theory of curriculum planning in primary art, craft and design education can be brought into closer correspondence with practice in a way that is 'accessible to teachers' (Stenhouse, 1975, p.112). There seems to have been a reluctance to do this, in this country at least, and Gentle points out that the literature in the particular field of primary art education has not yielded much in the way of 'an adequate theoretical rationale to guide practice appropriately and sensitively' (Gentle, 1981, p.20). Eisner suggests that some of the blame for this lies at the feet of those educators who see research in art as 'an uncomfortable intruder, somehow not belonging to the family of art' (Eisner, 1972a, p.237). There appears to exist an unease about using words in a field that is, above all things, visual. However, both Jeffrey (1980) and Kelsall (1980) state that, while perhaps the *artist* does not need to explain, the *art teacher* has a duty to communicate.

The particular rhetoric of the primary school itself has also in some measure militated against the definition of specific strategies, leading to a lack of any shared body of knowledge to support teachers in planning primary art, craft and design curricula (Sharp, 1984). Alexander suggests that this may be due to the pervasive philosophy that, in the primary school, we 'teach children, not subjects' (Alexander, 1984, p.15).

Indeed, few teachers would disagree that their major concern is for the individual development of each child. But it does not necessarily follow that, in the real world of the school, teachers should therefore absolve themselves of any responsibility for planning curricula and for addressing themselves to the matter of appropriate curriculum content.

What I am concerned with here is working towards a curriculum model that allows both for the development of the individual child and a respect for the fundamental epistemology of a particular area of knowledge and experience: in this case, art, craft and design. To this end, it would seem appropriate initially to consider what the literature has to say about building a core curriculum in art. It will then be seen how this may be applied to the primary classroom.

Read's approach
In 1943, Herbert Read proposed a model which identified three different aspects of art teaching:

1. self-expression;
2. observation;
3. appreciation.

The activity of self-expression (1), in Read's (1943) words, is to do with:

> the individual's innate need to communicate his thoughts, feelings and emotions to other people. (p.205)

The activity of observation (2) reflects:

> the individual's desire to record his sense impressions, to clarify his conceptual knowledge, to build up his memory, to construct things which aid his practical activities. (ibid.)

Appreciation (3) is:

> the qualitative reaction to the quantitative results of activities (1) and (2). (ibid.)

Read saw these three categories as distinct subjects, demanding separate and even unrelated methods of teaching. This point of view is questioned in the more recent literature.

Realms or domains of learning: Eisner and Allison

Eisner (1972a, 1972b), for instance, who also defines three categories of artistic learning, makes it clear that he considers them to be interrelated and interdependent. He identifies three 'realms' (1972a) or 'domains' (1972b):

1. the productive;
2. the critical; and
3. the cultural.

This approach foreshadows to a certain extent Allison's (1982) which identifies four 'domains':

1. the expressive/productive;
2. the perceptual;
3. the analytical/critical; and
4. the historical/cultural.

(i) *The productive realm/domain.* The productive realm, Eisner (1972a) explains, deals with the creation or making of art forms. It subsumes both an ability to observe and imagine and is concerned with the manipulation of materials so that they function as a medium of expression. Allison (1982) also sees this domain as being concerned with making and expression, although he is more explicit than Eisner (1972a) in his terminology. Eisner (1972a) maintains that the productive domain requires the ability to externalize invented schemes and to see the finished products as part of a greater configuration. The central point in this domain is defined by Eisner (1972a) as: 'realizing the cognitive perceptual complexity inherent in both the perception and creation of art' (p.106). Where Eisner (1972a) thus includes perception and creation (production) within the same category, Allison (1982) assigns each to a domain of its own.

(ii)   *The perceptual realm/domain.* Allison describes the perceptual domain as being charged with

> the development of skills which expand the capacities to see, feel and comprehend form, colour and texture as part of the encounter with the visual/tactile environment and which are fundamental to aesthetic experience (Allison, 1982, p.62)

(iii)   *The analytical/critical realm/domain.* Allison (1982) suggests that the critical realm should develop the skills of analysing, interpreting and evaluating aesthetic qualities in order to develop the capacities identified by Eisner (1972a) as being the concern of this realm: enjoying, experiencing and communicating about the content and form of art and design.

(iv)   *The historical/cultural realm/domain.* Eisner (1972a) emphasizes that the cultural realm, his third and final category, is essentially verbal in nature, although Allison (1982) takes a slightly different view. He asserts that recognition of historical/cultural meaning in art and design forms can be dependent upon the abilities fostered in the other domains of learning. This might imply that the historical/cultural domain need not be exclusively verbal. Both Eisner (1972a) and Allison (1982) agree that this realm/domain of learning concentrates on both the work of art and the artist in context as part of the cultural tradition, fostering an awareness of: 'the sweep of a period in human history and the rôle art (has) played within it' (Eisner, 1972a, p.232).

Summary of the realms/domains of learning. There does seem to be general agreement between Eisner (1972a) and Allison (1982) on the considerations which are embraced by these realms/domains. The main difference between the two writers is in the place given to aspects of perception: in Eisner's (1972a) model they are implied throughout the three domains, whereas in Allison's (1982) they are made more explicit and given a separate category. However, both writers insist that the realms/domains are only separated for clarity of communication and identification; in practice, they are 'unavoidably interdependent and inter-active with each other' (Allison, 1982, p.62).

Barrett's approach
In common with Allison (1982), Barrett (1979) draws attention to two

major issues that underlie the identification and development of a core curriculum in art. They are to do with: '(i) the essential nature of art [and] (ii) the rôle and purpose of art education' (Allison, 1982, p.61). Furthermore, Barrett (1979) also sees art education as consisting of three interrelated elements:

(i)   the personal and conceptual;
(ii) the operational; and
(iii) the synthetic.

The personal and conceptual element (i) is that aspect of art which 'operates through sensation, emotion, reminiscence, association, and inference' (p.5). The operational element (ii) is concerned with manipulating the materials of the environment using appropriate technical skills, so that the conceptual element is made manifest through the medium. The synthetic element (iii) is that aspect of art which relates to the visual elements as they are perceived: e.g. line, tone, colour, pattern, texture, form. Barrett explains it as 'the unified apprehension of the external world' (ibid., p.6).

These three categories are supported by the Schools Council (1978) who make them a little more accessible to the primary school teacher by referring to them as: 'The personal and conceptual element; the technical element; the visual element' (p.33). It is suggested by the Schools Council and Barrett that any one element may be taken as the starting point for a curriculum development project. However, it is understood that the three components are reflexive and interdependent, not existing discretely but in varying proportions as part of any visual inquiry.

Other approaches
Both the Gulbenkian Report (1982) and HMI (DES, 1984) see appreciation and participation as being mutually enriching strands in the pedagogical category of art teaching. Read himself acknowledges these twin aspects of learning in art by suggesting that the teacher might consider from two contrasting perspectives the curriculum s/he selects: '(i) the education of the individual as an artist, and (ii) the education of the individual in the appreciation of art' (Read, 1967, p.105). This view is also supported by Allison (1973, 1974).

Not only does a study of the literature reveal that appreciation and participation can be thought of as 'complementary aspects' of art education (Gulbenkian Report, 1982, p.41), but experience suggests that those participatory activities categorised by Read (1943) as 'observation' and 'self-expression' are also closely interdependent.

The Schools Council (1978), for example, far from separating the activities of observation and expression, believes that an objective study of the external world can help the child to nourish his/her inner world and so liberate his/her powers of self-expression. Within these activities of observation and expression, four interrelated categories or functions are identified:

recording and
analysis   } predominantly *objective* activities

communication and
expression.   } predominantly *subjective* activities

(For further explanation of these functions, see Schools Council *Art 7-11* (1978)

Gentle (1981) embraces both polarities — subjectivity and objectivity — when he argues that children's growth is dependent upon external control (i.e. over materials, objects and movements) and internal control (i.e. over responses and the capacity to absorb new experiences). The external control over materials involves a manifestation in concrete form of the internal control over responses: ideas are given form through media, which in turn generate further ideas and responses. The action is reflexive. However, if the child is not sensitive to change, this reflexive process will not take place.

Finally, it may be appropriate to conclude this consideration of the relationship between the internal and external worlds of the child by referring to Robertson's (1963) description of her own practice:

> I see the actual work to be done in the art 'lesson' as an alternation between the expression of direct spontaneous feeling with 'studies', more objective, deliberately undertaken exercises to explore the possibilities of the medium, to perfect some technique or representation. (Robertson, 1963, p.xxii)

To summarize this section dealing with the art curriculum models disclosed by the literature, Table 3.1 gives an overview of their fundamental orientations.

It can be seen that the models represented in Table 3.1 vary considerably in nature: some concentrate exclusively on defining the constituent parts of an art curriculum; others are concerned more with the kind of activities, methods or learning processes involved. Further,

Table 3.1: Models for the art curriculum
disclosed by the literature, in chronological order

Read **(1943)**	Self-expression;	Observation;	Appreciation
Robertson **(1963)**	Expression of direct, spontaneous feeling;		Deliberately undertaken (objective) studies
Read (1967) **Allison** **(1973, 1974)**	Child as artist;		Child as consumer
Eisner **(1972a)**	Productive;	Critical;	Cultural
Schools Council **(1978)**	Recording and Analysing (objective);		Expressing and Communi- cating (subjective)
Schools Council **(1978)**	Technical;	Visual;	Conceptual
Barrett **(1979)**	Synthetic;	Operational;	Conceptual
Gentle **(1981)**	External control;		Internal control
Allison **(1982)**	Expressive/ Productive;	Analytical/ Critical;	Perceptual; Cultural/ Historical
Gulbenkian Report **(1982)** **DES (1984)**	Participation;		Appreciation

there are those which combine method and content, the one being dependent upon the other. There does, however, appear to be much common ground upon which to formulate a specific model for use in the classroom.

Arriving at a specific model for the primary school
There is general agreement about what the constituent elements of a balanced art curriculum should be, although writers differ about how

these might be categorized. In their most straightforward terms, they are identified as: the technical element; the visual element; the conceptual element. It is emphasized by most of the writers that these elements are reflexive and on no account to be considered in isolation from each other.

A further point of agreement amongst educationists is that the productive aspect of art should be balanced by opportunities for appraisal and reflection. That is, there needs to be a balance of: 1. participation; and 2. appreciation.

Finally, within the art activitiy, whether the child is engaged in the process of making (participation) or appraising (appreciation), or a combination of both, it is essential that teachers are aware of the balance between: 1. subjective; and 2. objective experiences.

Thus, in summarizing the component elements of an appropriate primary art education, it can be said that there should be balance between: 1. technical, visual and conceptual elements; 2. appreciation and participation; 3. subjective and objective experiences.

Applying theory to practice: structuring a sequence of activities
In order to illustrate how the theory presented in the foregoing may be applied to a specific learning situation, I propose to use it to formulate a sequence of activities for implementation in the classroom.

In accordance with the advice from Barrett (1979) and the Schools Council (1978), one of the component elements of the art curriculum is taken as a starting point — in this case, the technical element — and in this specific example, it is intended to concentrate on the particular technique of painting.

The task in hand is how to make that area of knowledge and experience more meaningful to children at their own individual levels of development. For guidance in this, it may be useful to look at Bruner's (1960) pedagogical principles for the

> orderly and sequential teaching of any body of knowledge from the earliest years of schooling until those of maturity. (Edmonston, 1982, p.55)

These Brunerian principles, which Edmonston believes to be so relevant to teaching the visual arts are stated thus:

> (i)   any subject can be taught in some honest form to students at each stage of their development;

(ii) it is the task of the teacher to translate what is to be taught into the thought forms appropriate to the maturational level of the child or youth to be taught;

(iii) the subject should be taught at all levels in ways that make the underlying principles of a field of inquiry clear to the learner;

(iv) the school should not postpone the teaching of basic principles of a subject on the assumption that readiness to entertain principles is lacking on the part of the learner;

(v) it is probably easier to learn a discipline by behaving in ways similar to a mature practitioner .... than by doing something else;

(vi) modes of problem-solving which stress opportunity for student discovery of solutions should be stressed;

(vii) the end in view of teaching is the development of genuine student interest in learning and an appropriate set of attitudes toward intellectual activity in general, from the earliest days of schooling onward. (Edmonston's (1982) summary of Bruner's (1960) pedagogical principles)

This approach to building curricula has been described by Stenhouse (1975) as one possible means of structuring the process model for the curriculum, and providing an alternative for the objectives model. Both Barrett (1979) and Southworth (1980) favour the employment of the process model for art education, Southworth (1980) pointing out that there is 'a high degree of congruity between visual education and the process model' (p.44). Bearing in mind, then, the spirit of the process model, with its emphasis on learning by discovery from first-hand experiences and the opportunity for discussion and negotiation at all stages of the process (Blenkin and Kelly, 1981), the starting point for structuring this specific sequence of activities is to decide upon what the underlying principles of painting might be.

The three curricular elements — the technical, the visual and the conceptual — are used to categorize these principles.

The technical element
Smith (1983) in her definition of the periods of growth discernible in children's painting activity, gives the first one as that representing the need to master the medium. Carline (1968) and Gentle (1985) suggest that this can be done by experimentation and exploration.

The basic requirements of this technical element in the primary school are: 1. paint; 2. paper; 3. brushes. 1. *Paint*. It is necessary for children to understand the qualities of paint: its varying consistencies, strengths and drying times and its mixing properties. 2. *Paper*. Children can be given opportunities to discover which kind of paper is most suitable for the kind of paint they are using. 3. *Brushes*. Children need to be made aware of the variety of brushes available, and to have the opportunity to discover which brush is most appropriate for a particular purpose.

The visual element
The most obvious visual elements employed in the technique of painting are colour and tone, although many others are also embraced: e.g. pattern, texture, shape, point, line and form. Carline advocated that colour mixing should be the first consideration of a study of colour, and that it is often wisest to let the beginner experiment in any way s/he chooses (Carline, 1968, p.211). Colour-mixing games, such as those invented by Richardson (1948) and Jameson (1971) can also be employed in order to develop colour perception and to give practice in identifying colour. A limited palette comprising only primary colours (red, blue and yellow) with the addition of black and white may help promote extensive experimentation.

Figure 3.1: Experimenting with various kinds of brush

The tone (lightness or darkness) of a colour can also be considered and discussed, although this may be a more difficult concept for younger children.

The conceptual element

A strong feeling emerges from the literature that, while it is essential for children to learn skills, mastery of them is not a prerequisite of being allowed to work expressively. Skills and technique are a means to an end, not ends in themselves (Best, 1979). It is therefore necessary that children be allowed to use what skills they have at their disposal to 'behave like painters' (if we accept the Brunerian principle) and to make pictures. Richardson (1948) and Reid (1967) both shared the view that only by *being* an artist can an individual be acquainted with the concepts and meanings embodied in art.

Within the sequence of activities, if there is to be a proper balance of the elements identified earlier, then there must be acknowledgment of two other issues, viz: balance between appreciation and participation; and balance between subjective and objective experiences.

Appreciation and participation

So far, the activities described have been concerned mainly with making art, or participating in the art activity. However, built into the proposed sequence of activities must be the stipulation that children are given opportunities to reflect upon and appraise their own work, the work of their peers and the work of artists. These opportunities will have two functions: 1. to enable children to evaluate their progress, and so to help shape future activities; and 2. to encourage them to see their own place as artists within the broad continuum of an established tradition and an evolving culture.

Subjective and objective experiences

It is often difficult to distinguish between these orientations in practice: usually it is the case that children, depending on their developmental levels, combine both orientations in differing proportions within the same experience. However, to ensure that children are given the visual support advocated by the Schools Council (1979, 1981), the sequence of activities will provide opportunities to work from direct observation of their surroundings. The degree to which their subjective imagery is influenced will be dependent on their stage of development in painting.

Having determined the most important constituent elements for the sequence of activities, it is now intended to define the aim of the sequence, and then to open out this aim into a set of pedagogical principles.

Aim and pedagogical principles of the sequence of activities
The aim is to introduce children to the fundamental disciplines and characteristics of painting.
  The pedagogical principles are as follows:

1. to promote an understanding of the qualities and limitations of paint as a medium and painting as a technique;
2. to develop in children skills and, consequently, confidence in using paint by providing appropriate learning experiences;
3. to facilitate expression through the promotion of the specific skills to be taught;
4. to develop visual perception;
5. to support the child's own individual imagery with relevant visual source material and discussion;
6. to give children opportunities to reflect upon their experiences;
7. to encourage children to make judgements about their work and the work of their peers;
8. to encourage children to relate their own responses to those of professional artists by looking at and discussing paintings, or reproductions of paintings; and
9. to begin to develop a critical vocabulary in children.

An overview of the proposed sequence of activities is now followed by a more detailed account of how the sequence was implemented in a particular school.

Overview of the sequence
The sequence is composed of eight sessions, each of about one and a half hours in duration. The first two sessions are intended to provide material for the participating children to make appropriate formative evaluations which will then shape the course for future activities. The final session allows for a summative evaluation of the entire sequence (Figures 3.2 and 3.3).

Session 1:   Children, working in pairs, are to be asked to paint a portrait of each other, with no stimulation or guidance from the teacher. At the end of this session, all portraits (finished and unfinished) are to be displayed. Children are

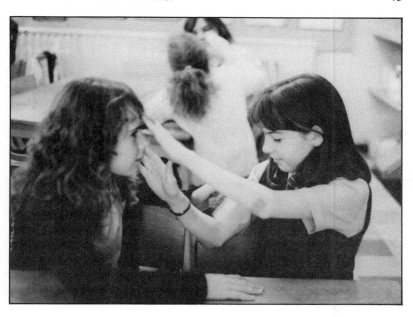

Figure 3.2 (above): Preliminary work for children's drawings of each other

Figure 3.3 (below): Learning to look: pencil drawing from close and careful observation

to be given time to view them all, and then to discuss any difficulties they may have encountered or to make any relevant observations.

Session 2:   Children, in groups of four to six, are to discuss a collection of six postcard reproductions of paintings of people. In the light of this discussion, children are to look again at the portraits they have painted and to identify ways in which they might be modified.

Sessions 3,   The content of these will depend upon the formative
4 and 5:   evaluations made by children in Session 2. Activities will be designed to accommodate the problems and opportunities identified.

Session 6   Working in the same pairs as in Session 1, children
and 7:   are to paint portraits of each other from direct observation. This time, the teacher is to intervene as considered appropriate.

Session 8:   Summative evaluation; children are to compare their first and second paintings and to be asked which they prefer and why. They are then to be given the opportunity to view all the work done by the whole class over the duration of the eight-week period.

Implementing the sequence in the classroom
What follows is an account of the outcomes of the sequence of activities as implemented in the classroom, with a group of 28 children of mixed ability, aged 9 - 11 years. (The catchment area of the school contains a fairly close-knit Welsh community, where there is only minimal presence of other ethnic groups.)

Session 1

PURPOSE OF THE SESSION	MATERIALS/ EQUIPMENT	CONTENT/ METHODOLOGY
To achieve an untutored painting, to be used by pupils as a basis for	Paints: red, blue, yellow, purple, white, black.	In pairs, children are to paint each other from direct observation.

discussion and identification of problems. Also to be used as a criterion against which to judge the final painting.	Brushes: hog's hair, fine-tipped nylon (various sizes). Paper: A3 size white cartridge.	No stimulus or guidance is given by the teacher. At the end of the session children discuss the work and identify problems.

Outcomes of Session 1

It was noted that the entire class chose to draw the portrait first in pencil. This preliminary drawing was, in most cases, executed in some detail, even down to freckles and eyelashes, before any paint was applied. These details were then obliterated by the paint which, the children complained, 'spoiled' their drawings. The knowledge that they were about to paint had not modified their approach to the task. This fact may have been due to lack of experience with paint: the class had not been accustomed to having regular opportunities to paint during the three or four years spent in the junior school.

At the end of the first session, a class discussion revealed the following problems: (i) mixing colours for skin and hair was difficult; (ii) colours were running together because the paint was wet; (iii) getting the 'right shape' was difficult; (iv) brushes were too thick to 'get into little places'; (v) not enough time to finish.

Session 2

PURPOSE OF THE SESSION	MATERIALS/ EQUIPMENT	CONTENT/ METHODOLOGY
To study and discuss postcard reproductions of paintings of people; in the light of this discussion, to look again at the portraits painted by the children – how might they be modified?	6 packs of 6 postcard reproductions: Cézanne, 'Self-portrait'; Degas, 'Elena Carafa'; Ghirlandaio, 'Portrait of a Girl'; Botticelli, 'Portrait of a Young Man'; Duccio, 'Virgin' and Child,	In groups of 5, children are given opportunity to look at and discuss postcards. Then, their attention was focused by the teacher onto certain things: e.g. background, clothes, colours, 'mood' and personality of sitter, brush strokes, etc. Children then look

Matisse, 'Portrait of again at their own
Greta Moll'   portraits and are asked
how they might be
improved, if at all.

The postcard reproductions provided examples of European painting from the twelfth century to the early twentieth century, showing a variety of styles ranging from the early iconographic painting by Duccio to the bold, flat, patterned statement of Matisse. The subjects of the paintings were varied in character, age and sex and were judged to have a particular appeal for children.

Outcomes of Session 2
After the discussion session in which children's attention was focused on the postcard reproductions, they made the following suggestions as to how they might modify their own paintings. They said that next time they would: 1. paint a background (none of them had in the previous session); 2. try and mix more accurately the colours they see; 3. think of the order in which they might paint, e.g. details would be painted last, and large areas would be painted first; 4. some of the paint should be allowed to dry before painting over it.

Sessions 3, 4 and 5
As a result of the formative evlautions made by the children in Sessions 1 and 2, it was decided to use Sessions 3, 4 and 5 to promote skills in: 1. colour perception and colour mixing; 2. the use of various kinds of brushes; 3. observational drawing. Session 3 was devoted to colour-mixing exercises and games, encouraging the matching of colour. Session 4 gave children opportunities to use a variety of brushes in an expressive way, first by experimenting in mark-making and then by making with the brushes large-scale linear drawings of some grasses the children had collected. Session 5 concentrated on encouraging children to make carefully-observed pencil drawings of each other, with some initial drama work to stimulate focused looking.

Sessions 6 and 7

PURPOSE OF THE SESSIONS	MATERIALS/ EQUIPMENT	CONTENT/ METHODOLOGY
To paint a second portrait capitalizing	As for Session 1	Children are asked to paint a second portrait; they

upon the experiences provided over the previous sessions. Two sessions are given to this activity, so that children may, if they wish, leave the painting to dry at a certain stage before completing it.

are reminded of Session 2 and the observations they had made. They are asked to consider the following:

1. What exactly am I going to paint today?
2. What are the things I am going to leave until next time?
3. Do I need to do any drawing first?
4. What is the least amount of drawing I need to do?

Outcomes of Session 6
Discussion of the four points outlined above resulted in general agreement about some of the strategies to be adopted in carrying out the second painting. These were as follows: (i) the main concern of this session would be to establish the basic shape of the head and shoulders, and to carefully match the skin and hair colour. The basis for a background would also be fixed. (ii) Details of features, etc., would be left until next time. (iii) Some children thought it would be a good idea to use a brush instead of a pencil for the initial basic drawing. They felt that this might discourage an over-concern with detail at this stage.

Outcomes of Session 7
In a preliminary discussion, children were given the opportunity to look at all the paintings begun in the previous session. They were asked if they could remember all the points that had been raised by the discussions in the first two sessions. After these had been considered, pupils were advised to give further thought to the order in which they intended to complete their paintings.

It was necessary to remind some of the less confident children how to mix certain colours, by referring back to the activities of the earlier sessions. All children were given as much time as they needed to finish the portrait to their satisfaction.

Final session

PURPOSE OF THE SESSION	MATERIALS/ EQUIPMENT	CONTENT/ METHODOLOGY
To review the whole course and to give children the opportunity to make a summative evaluation of the sequence of activities.	All the work by the children to be displayed	Children are given time to look at all the work done during the past 7 sessions, and encouraged to inspect and reflect upon their own work and that of their peers. They are asked to bear in mind the following considerations;

CONTENT/ METHODOLOGY (continued):

1. Which of your two portraits do you prefer?
2. What reasons do you have for your answer?
3. What do you think you have learned from the course?

Outcomes of final session

Two-thirds of the class thought that their second paintings were better than their first. The children who preferred their first paintings did so because they felt that the drawing was 'more realistic'. They were only able to judge the work from the criterion of visual realism. It was difficult for them to understand the fundamental difference between a painted drawing and a painting *per se*.

Children who preferred their second paintings gave reasons such as:

Because I put more detail.

My first time I didn't have enough time.

Because I got the colour of hair and skin nearer the real colour.

Because I drew the first painting before painting it.

I think the second portrait has better shades of colour, and a better shape and the hair has better brush strokes.

Because it had a background.

Because the second one had more thought put into it.

In response to the question, What do you think you have learned from the course? One child said he had not learned anything. The others gave comments which are typified below:

> I learned to mix colours and to get the right shape.
> I have learned how to use a brush better.
> I have learned something, not to paint it all the same time.
> I have learned to control the brush better.
> I have learned a bit. I've learned how to set about painting a portrait.
> I have learned not to just do the outline, but do the colour of the face as well.
> I have learned the shape and colour of hair and skin.

My own judgement of the second paintings was that almost all of them were more 'painterly' in quality: that is, they were more than simply coloured-in drawings, which the first portraits had been.

I felt that the aim of the sequence of activities had been fulfilled, but in varying degrees.

Commentary

The sequence of activities which I have described here was carefully structured and planned, but allowed for individual responses from the participating children in order to shape further activities. It was possible in the planning stage to anticipate, within certain limits, what these responses might be and consequently to be prepared for possible future developments.

The rôle of the teacher in the art activity is not easy to define: it has been the subject of some controversy. My own tendency is to go along with current thinking, that the teacher's rôle is more positive than has been advocated in the past by such influential educators as Lowenfeld (see, for instance, Southworth, 1981, Eisner, 1982, and Smith, 1982).

Some readers may argue that the teacher's rôle in the sequence of activities described here has been too assertive, too overt. I argue that it has given children the security of a framework within which to operate, thus enabling them to develop technical skills and to express themselves to a degree which, if left to their own devices, they would be unlikely to achieve. As Whitehead (in Donaldson, 1978) put it:

> the child is the heir to long ages of civilization and it is absurd to let him wander in the intellectual maze of men in the Glacial Epoch. (p.119)

The two main strands (of participation and appreciation) contributing to the structure of these activities have been caught in a reflexive relationship between doing (or making) and thinking about, talking about, reflecting upon, art. The use of realized form (as Witkin, 1974, calls it) is incidental, synthesized into the activity, so that children learn to relate their own direct experiences of the world to those of other, established, artists and craftspersons. For some reason, the use of realized form does not seem to have been as widely implemented in visual art education as it has been in the case of the other arts. Most people would agree, for instance, that it would be unusual for a teacher to expect children to write poems without first having had the opportunity to listen to or read poems. How else would a child know what a poem was? Or that there were different kinds of poems? Similarly, then, children can learn from the way visual artists have coped with problems similar to their own:

How do you paint grass? (How many different ways?)
How do you draw noses?
How do you decorate a clay pot?

The philosophy governing the series of activities given here as an example of operationalizing educational theory is set squarely in the Western European painting tradition. This seemed to me an appropriate place to start (but *only* to start) with a homogeneous class of Welsh children. It is an old educational cliché, but I think true, that we begin from where we are. But we do not need to stop there. An extension of this study of the face, for instance, might be to look at ways in which it is depicted by other cultures, from the African tribal mask to the North American Indian totem pole. Further, this would provide an opportunity for children to work in other media and dimensions, complementing the experiences with paint in two dimensions already gained.

We need not be bound by a picture of culture that, in the words of the Gulbenkian Report (1982, p.38), encompasses 'a comparatively narrow range of work favoured by particular sections of one culture – [our] own'. The most important thing, it would seem, is to try and maintain a balance

between the ostensibly conflicting demands of a central tradition, cultural innovation and the assimilation and conservation of diverse models and practices. (Simpson, 1986, p.152)

Dyson, elsewhere in this volume (and in Dyson, 1986), agrees that these demands need not be conflicting, and invokes Gombrich's argument that one's cultural roots can be explored in the context of an awareness of world culture. Clearly, though, teachers need to be aware of the highly sensitive issues in this educational mine-field; guidance is needed and probably, as Allison (1986) urges, in-service training.

Conclusion

It has been with some reluctance that I have recorded here actual practice in the classroom. The more I read and reflect, the more I wonder that I have the temerity to teach. Yet I still firmly believe that, if the reality and the rhetoric of the primary school are to become one, there is a need for teachers to rationalize practice and to communicate it to others. Otherwise, theory and practice will be a constant dichotomy.

References

Alexander, R.J. (1984), *Primary Teaching*. Eastbourne: Holt Reinhart Winston.

Allison, B. (1973), 'Sequential programming in art education', in D.W. Piper (ed.), *Readings in Art and Design Education: after Hornsey*. London: Davis-Poynter, pp.59-68.

—————————— (1974), 'Professional art education', *National Society for Art Education (NSAE) Journal*. February 1974, pp.3-8.

—————————— (1982), 'Identifying the core in art and design', *Journal of Art and Design Education*. Vol.1, No.1, pp.59-66.

—————————— (1986), 'Cultural dimensions of art and design', *Journal of Art and Design Education*. Vol.4, No.3, pp.217-223.

Barrett, M. (1979), *Art Education: a strategy for course design*. London: Heinemann Educational Books.

Best, D. (1979), 'Free expression or the teaching of techniques?' *British Journal of Educational Studies*. Vol.xxvii, No.3.

Blenkin, G. and Kelly, A.V. (1981), *The Primary Curriculum*. London: Harper & Row.

Bruner, J.C. (1960), *The Process of Education*. Cambridge Mass: Harvard University Press.

Carline, R. (1968), *Draw They Must: a history of the teaching and examining of art*. London: Arnold.

Department of Education and Science (1984), *Curriculum and Organization of Primary Schools in Wales, Education Issues 7*, Welsh Office. London: HMSO.

Donaldson, M. (1978), *Children's Minds*. London: Fontana.

Dyson, A. (1986), 'The three-card trick: the reading of images by young children', *Journal of Art and Design Education*. Vol.5, Nos.1 and 2, pp.69-80.

Edmonston, P. (1982), 'A rationale, for a curriculum in the visual arts', *Journal of Art and Design Education*. Vol.1, No.1, pp.47-57.

Eisner, E.W. (1972a), *Educating Artistic Vision*. New York: Macmillan.

_____ (1972b), 'Emerging models for educational evaluation', *School Review, North American Journal of Education*, Vol.80, No.4.

_____ (1982), 'The relationship of theory and practice', *Art Education*. Vol.35, No.1, pp.4-5.

Gentle, K. (1981), 'The development of children's art', *Education 3-13*. Vol.9, No.2.

_____ (1985), *Children and Art Teaching*. Teaching 5 - 13 Series. London: Croom Helm.

Gulbenkian Report (1982), *The Arts in Schools*. London: Gulbenkian Foundation.

Jameson, K. (1971), *Junior School Art*. London: Studio Vista.

Jeffrey, R. (1980), 'Assessment in the arts', in *Creative Arts in the Secondary School*. Report of a Conference organized by HMI (Wales) 1980.

Kelsall, R.T. (1980), 'Time for a change of thinking: a reply', *National Society for Art Education Journal* (NSAE), Vol.vii, No.3, pp.14-18.

Read, H. (1943), *Education through Art*. London: Faber & Faber.

_____ (1967), *Art and Society*. Fourth Edn. London: Faber & Faber.

Reid, L.A. (1967), *Meaning in the Arts*. London: Allen & Unwin.

Richardson, M. (1948), *Art and the Child*. London: University of London Press.

Robertson, S. (1963), *Rosegarden and Labyrinth*. London: Routledge.

Schools Council (1978), *Art 7 - 11*, Occasional Bulletin from the Subjects Committee. London: Schools Council.

——————— (1981), *Resources for Visual Education 7 - 13*, Occasional Bulletin from the Subjects Committee. London: Schools Council.

Sharp, P. (1984), 'Uncritical, unconfident, uncommunicative', *Arts Express*. July 1984, pp.8-9.

Simpson, A. (1986), 'Multiculture and art: paradoxical and unstable concepts', *Journal of Art and Design Education*. Vol.5, Nos.1 and 2, pp.143-154.

Smith, N. (1982), 'The visual arts in early childhood education. Development of the creation of meaning', in B. Spodek (ed.), *Handbook of Research in Early Childhood Education*. New York. Free Press.

——————— (1983), 'Experience and art', *Teaching Children to Paint*. New York: Teachers College Press.

Southworth, G. (1980), 'The curriculum process model and its implications for visual education in the primary sector'. Unpublished MEd thesis. University of Liverpool.

——————— (1981), 'The process of teaching art in primary schools', *Education 3 - 13*. Vol.9, No.2, pp.25-26.

Stenhouse, L.A. (1975), *An Introduction to Curriculum Research and Development*. London: Heinemann Educational Books.

Stumbo, H.W. (1970), 'Three bases for research and teaching in the arts: subjective, objective and projective', In G. Pappas (ed.), *Concepts in Art and Education*. London: Macmillan.

Witkin, R.W. (1974), *The Intelligence of Feeling*. London: Heinemann Educational Books.

Chapter Four
Making and Playing, the Other Basic Skills: design education for the early years
Vera Coghill

Design education for the early school years is an undervalued and neglected curriculum area. Yet arguments can be put forward for seeing design capability as fundamental in human understanding and so as basic a skill as literacy and numeracy (Baynes, 1985; Coghill, 1986). Initially, design capability is made manifest through the making and playing of early childhood. This making and playing is itself skilful activity, which can be enhanced and extended or else discouraged. I see making and playing, the early indicators of design capacity and capability, as the other basic skills ranking in importance with the more traditional ones.

By tradition the early school years are the time when the ground work is done in the basic skills of literacy, numeracy and social and physical competence. More recently, subject specialists in music, science, technology, art and environmental studies have wanted to ensure that their disciplines are equally well covered in the early schooling of every child. This is not, however, a plea to have a subject called 'design' represented in the curriculum of the young child; design capability is not subject – specific and, in fact, encompasses all of the specialist areas mentioned above. Rather, this is a plea for a recognition and reassessment of its potential in the development of children's intellectual powers.

Basic skills are usually seen as being embedded in 'learning by doing' which, itself, has a tradition in early schooling almost as strong as that of the three Rs. Activities are a part of the accepted procedure in educational practice for the young. But comparatively little attention has been paid recently to just what it is children are doing when involved in activity-based learning. Even in the first school years a separation exists in many schools between activities seen as work and those thought to be play. Making and playing are often viewed as the means, or vehicle, for learning other things rather than as activities valuable in themselves. They are often seen as the sugar to coat the bitter pill of learning, as a tonic to revive flagging spirits, or as a reward for working. They are not regarded as skilful in their own right nor as fundamental human intellectual tools.

This division of the early school curriculum into 'work' and those activities thought of as 'play', often designated 'creative activities', is acknowledged in contemporary accounts of early schooling, where it is seen as the norm. Mary Willes (1983) in her study of language in early schooling found that 'creative activities' were seen as a particular kind of task, usually involving making and playing, and were confined to separate periods of time during the day. An article in *The Times Educational Supplement* on the admission of nursery children to infant classes highlights this distinction between work and play:

> And there is plenty of evidence that the normal infant regime — with its clear distinction between 'work' and 'play' and its emphasis on 'basic skills' in the morning and 'creative' work in the afternoon — is not being adapted to suit the youngest children. (*The Times Educational Supplement*, 17 May, 1985)

It is not only the youngest children but all children who are being penalized by a system which does not recognize making and playing as basic life skills which encompass design capacity, awareness and capability.

Design capacity, awareness and capability

The word 'design' is used here in an active sense. It is not used to denote the configuration of an artefact or system but rather to define the actions and activities, thoughts, feelings, imaginings and understandings one brings to bear upon the fashioning or imagining of an artefact or system. It has to do with taking action and with imagining and considering what actions could or might be taken. In designing, the intention is to re-order, change, or alter spatial or physical reality for a specific purpose or idea.

Design capacity allows one to act physically with intention upon materials and objects, or to have ideas and thoughts about such actions. It enables one to order and change things according to one's ideas of how they could or might be. Thus, one orders and changes the environment to suit one's feelings, needs, ideas or whims of what the world, or part of it anyway, could or should or might be like. The ability to order into patterns, sequences and structures seems to be an innate human characteristic (Gombrich, 1979). So is the making of choices and evaluations which do not necessarily depend upon words. Lethaby (1921) says we are all designers. He saw the designer as 'the explorer, the experimenter, the inventor', as someone not content to take things just as they are but whose special faculty is to wonder how things would be if 'like this' or 'like that'.

Design awareness is the kind of knowing in which the individual using cognitive models and maps, ideas and representations, imagines and considers the possibilities of action directed towards some, as yet, not fully perceived end. It could be called the 'what if' or 'suppose' syndrome and it requires something more than unfettered imagination, intuition or thought. It is the way in which people make meaning through action or imagined action. As this capacity develops and grows it encompasses knowledge and insight into the awareness of the designed environment. Through such awareness one is able to take on, or take in, the knowledge and meanings implicit in the artefacts and systems of the particular environment in which one finds oneself.

Design capability is the degree to which the individual extends and develops an innate design capacity. It can be compared to language. Language development depends upon both an innate capacity for language, a part of the neurological make up, and the use and exercise of a gradually increasing competence in language. So, I believe, does design capability depend upon the structures which underlie design capacity together with an increasing sophistication and emergence of the ability to order and rearrange physical or spatial reality. Design capacity includes the management of change. Play is the skilled activity in which this management is practised. Orders are created and destroyed in the service of an idea or cluster of ideas.

Characteristics and function of play

Human play arises out of the capacity to make bridges imaginatively between our own inner reality and the reality which is outside ourselves (Winnicott, 1958, 1971). In this juxtaposition of inner and outer reality there exists for a time a negotiation between, a spanning of, these two modes of perceiving: from inside out and from outside in; the two realities become one as they are fused in play. Winnicott tells us that the child playing demonstrates a preoccupation and concentration akin to that of older children and adults, that the area of play lies neither in inner nor outer reality, but in a sphere or space of its own. He also notes how the child gathers objectives and phenomena from 'external reality' and uses them in the service of 'some sample derived from inner or personal reality' into which the child 'puts out a sample of dream potential and lives with this sample in a chosen setting of fragments from external reality' (Winnicott, 1971, p.60).

Winnicott sees this as a direct development from the use by babies of a 'transitional object' to take the place of the mother (Winnicott, 1958). Into objects and materials the child interjects what Winnicott terms a 'dream potential'. Thus the object becomes a part of the space, or sphere, between inner and outer reality in which play happens. It is this ability to give things *outside* personal reality a space *inside* it and a dream potential (which while recognized as 'real' is nevertheless not real life) that equates well with design thinking. Through play the child is an extraordinary designer.

In his comprehensive work on play Huizinga (1949) gives as its three main characteristics: that it is free, that it is, indeed, freedom; that it is not 'ordinary' or 'real' life, but is, rather, a stepping out of 'real' life into a temporary sphere of activity with a disposition all its own; that it is distinct from 'ordinary' life both as to locality and duration. He goes on to give a function of play: it creates order, indeed it *is* order.

We play because we want to play, but in this play we create an order that exists *because we say it is so* or *because we have arranged it so*. Is this not also what the designer does? I think Huizinga's statement of the function of play shows how play and design are related concepts. The following example of children playing in school from my 1978 classroom journal illustrates the creation of such order:

On a recent occasion I was watching a group of five year olds at play in school. They had a rather old balance-beam which they were using in their game of 'shops'. This was a conventional beam with twenty hooks — ten on each side of the fulcrum. The original washers were lost and the children were using some Formica pattern tiles to hang on the hooks; there were plenty of these so that even with the beam full there were plenty of spare tiles. One child acted as shopkeeper; he was in charge of the balance beam. This he used alternatively as display shelf and till. A child would come to the shop holding some tiles as money. He'd say something like, 'I want potatoes'. The shopkeeper then asked, 'How much money have you got?' The customer then counted out a number of his money tiles and handed them over to the shopkeeper. The shopkeeper took them, counted them and put them down on the table and turned to his display shelf (the balance beam), took that number of tiles off the hook, handed them to the customer, 'Here's your potatoes', picked up the money tiles from the table and hung them on the beam on the hooks vacated by the goods; the beam now appears to be functioning as a till. The shopkeeper then turned to the next customer. This game went on for many minutes. Finally another child took over as shopkeeper. He played for a few minutes in a similar manner. Then, during one transaction he merely took the tile money from the customer and, without going through the motions of counting it, placing it on the table, taking goods from the shelf and then putting the money in the till, he just handed the original money tiles back to the customer as goods. There were immediate cries of, 'It's not fair', 'You're cheating'.*

These children were engaged in a social activity which can clearly be recognized as play. They had invested objects from external reality with a 'dream potential' which enabled them to devise a structure, or system, through which the play happened. These props became the focus around which order was imposed. Some activities are less easily seen to be play. Sometimes play is solitary, or individual, and may involve no observable activity.

Play is largely an attitude of mind or a feeling. Brenda Crowe (1983) in her delightful book *Play is a Feeling* maintains that 'real play springs from within us'. She recognizes and deplores the way in which adults take over children's play and turn it into a 'play situation' in the interests of developing linguistic or intellectual competence. There is a failure on the part of many parents, teachers and psychologists to recognize the intrinsic worth of play and the fact that real play is the source of both meaning and being. Arising as it does from a space between inner and outer reality it belongs to our own self in a way no other activity can.

The elusive nature of play makes it difficult to study. Garvey (1977) contrasts 'playful' and 'non-playful' versions of the same activity and concludes that play is more of an attitude than any particular kind of behaviour. This accords well with the notion of play as a feeling. Yet, Garvey takes a very narrow view of the sorts of activities which she sees as play. She disallows as play the very forms of play which may be the

---

* Quoted by Walkerdine and Sinha in 'Developing linguistic strategies', G. Wells (ed.), 1983, pp.197-8. They comment: 'It is interesting to note the way in which the rules for the game are generated here. The game was certainly not being played in a haphazard way, but rather specific rules were formulated by the participants, which utilized the particular "props" that were available in the situation.'

most intrinsically satisfying and which in the long term are most beneficial for the player.

Garvey gives five charactersitics of play: it is pleasurable; it has no intrinsic goals, is an enjoyment of means rather than effort devoted to some end and as such is inherently unproductive; it is spontaneous and voluntary; it involves active engagement on the part of the player; and it has certain systematic relations to what is non-play. I have no real argument with these characteristics of play. They correspond with both Winnicott's and Huizinga's view that play arises from within, is freedom, and its function is the creation of order. It is with Garvey's interpretations that I disagree. These have far-reaching implications when considering the place of play in the young child's schooling.

Garvey bases her study on the assumption that play has certain systematic relations to what is not play. This is not so much a characteristic of play itself as of play as it is viewed by a researcher or other outsider. The person playing may pass freely back and forth between 'play' and 'not play' as a part of the same activity or action. We, those who are outside the play, cannot be sure whether what we observe is or is not play. Play is, at some level, always a private activity which cannot be systematized nor scrutinized. Garvey also asserts that to be classed as play an activity must be necessarily 'unproductive'. In doing so she disallows as play activity and action which others like Winnicott and Huizinga would clearly perceive as being play.

It seems to me that Garvey has been caught by the 'researcher's trap' — if an activity cannot be observed and quantified it is not happening. She disallows 'work or artistic endeavours' which may be pleasurable and spontaneous because they have an end product and are intended to change the world in some perceptible way. She does not include 'daydreaming' since, although it is conceived as pleasurable and voluntary, she sees it as passive. I believe that activity in play can be mental as well as physical. Daydreaming may be an enriched mental activity in which all sorts of 'new orders' are allowed to steam away unabated and out of which the dreamer creates original thoughts and plays with them in yet more patterns. Whether an activity is called 'work' or 'play' may depend as much upon semantics as upon observation, upon feeling more than intellect, upon attitude more than research.

In addition the child building a sand castle, baking cakes, playing with clay or wood, painting, etc., is often as interested in 'the product' as any artist or artisan. The play does often intend to 'change the world' in some perceptible way. Garvey sees as 'not play' any activity which is

directed towards an objective other than itself. Whilst the 'enjoyment of
means', as she puts it, is of paramount importance — that is, it is the
process that counts as play — there is often a *product* which is of
immense importance to the conduct of the play and without which the
play would not have happened. It is the product which often acts as a
container for the various elements of the play, and which may constitute
the purpose of the play. The purpose cannot be separated from the
actions. It is not that a play activity must be necessarily "unproductive'
to count as play, but that the product must belong to the purpose of the
play and hence be of importance to the player. In taking over the
purpose of play, which happens in school often times with an undue
emphasis upon a preconceived product, the activity is rendered void as a
play activity.

Dorothy Einon (1985) provides a handbook for parents on 'play with
a purpose' in which she reveals a rather instrumental concept of play.
All of the ages and stages of childhood are laid out with the appropriate
play activity listed and tabulated with procedures and purposes of the
play provided. It is rather like a recipe book for getting a child through
childhood. Surely all play has a purpose. The purpose is a part of the
play and belongs to the player. The prescriptive and rather clinical
nature of Einon's advice belies this ownership of play, that which makes
it the creation of the player. By seeing play as a means to something else,
by removing the purpose of play from the actions of the play itself,
Einon invites exploitation of the child and its feelings. She encourages
outside intervention in what is a private and personal activity. This is
reinforced by the fact that she attributes a value to each play activity as
if this extrinsic worth is the measure by which play ought to be valued.
This is exactly the position taken up by those teachers who see play as a
means to other intellectual ends rather than as a valid, skilled
intellectual activity in its own right.

Learning and play

It is through play that the child makes meaning. Susan Isaacs (1930)
recognized the value of the child's imagination as an aid to intellectual
growth. The relationship between fantasy life and an active intellectual
interest in the world of real events and things was seen as a principle for
curriculum development during the nineteen-thirties largely because of
Isaacs' influence (Board of Education, 1931, 1933). What makes her
work of interest even now is her recognition of the need for something
more than 'self-expression' in the arts, and that she saw reading and

writing as more than just tools. Her commitment was to children and to play as an intellectual activity. This play encompassed both a delight in the world of imagination and drama and the 'finding out' about the physical world which children experienced in their environment. She saw no separation between work and play.

Recognition of play as an intellectual tool was a feature of the Plowden Report (1967) where the child as an agent in his or her own learning was clearly acknowledged. In the era following this report there was much foolishness and misunderstanding about the role of play in education. Because many teachers were not aware of the nature and function of play, licence was sometimes confused with freedom by both teachers and children, bad and lazy practice was sometimes disguised as 'self-expression'. In addition, since play is not something which can be measured and evaluated in the way more controlled activities can, it is viewed with suspicion in an educational climate which demands 'standards' of practice and evaluation of even the youngest child's work. Yet, play is valuable, even essential, in itself. Through it one exercises the skill of adapting physical reality to conform with an image of what that reality might be. Playing is a means of bringing into focus the world as it is, together with the world as it might be. So is designing.

This capacity to act upon the environment is present in the youngest infant. Initially, learning arises almost incidentally out of the infant's need for action to satisfy physiological and psychological demands. These, together with the caregiver's attentive interpretation of the infant's wishes and the expectations each create in the other, allow for a situation in which the infant is able to order experiences. As the child grows less dependent upon the caregiver, curiosity becomes the spur for meaning-making. This curiosity is often embedded in action or activity centred upon an object or plaything into which a 'dream potential' is projected. Such object play is often associated with 'learning by doing'.

To understand the potential of 'learning by doing' as an educational principle it may be helpful to rearrange the slogan to read: 'Because we do, we learn'. We are, thus, seen as active agents in our own meaning-making. An emphasis placed upon the fact that 'we do and so we learn' focuses attention upon the private and egocentric nature of much learning itself. We *make* meanings. Although much early learning is tied to developmental growth, the particular way in which a given infant develops depends, too, upon the kind and quality of experience he or she has. These experiences reflect not only the child's social and environmental reality but also the actions and consequences of actions arising from within the child's innermost being. The meanings which are made encompass both the experience and the experiencing of the experience together with the actions or activity in which the experience is embedded. These meanings are often embedded in, or projected into, aspects of physical reality which act as holders for the thoughts and actions so that they can be contemplated, worked upon or changed. It is through this kind of play that design awareness is nurtured and design capability extended. I call this kind of intellectual activity, or meaning-making, 'introspective play'.

In such play the child engages in a conversation between inner and outer reality by using materials and objects from external reality as props in an internal dialogue. Concentration and commitment to task are the most potent features of such introspective play. Adults deep in concentration, trying to work through an idea, demonstrate the same sort of commitment to an internal reality. Ideas may be realized by 'making things', by rendering or by wroughting and by changing properties of the environment to conform with an internal notion of 'nearness of fit'. It is particularly a feature of design thinking. One might call such introspection 'designerly play'. Such concentration on and commitment to task is one of the skills necessary throughout life. When one talks of the transfer of skills as an educational aim, concentration, involvement in and commitment to a task emerge as amongst the most crucial.

Designerly play in the early years
In some schools and by some teachers, there is an active embracing of learning through designerly play. The child is seen as an agent of his or her own learning and a commitment to task is fostered. This is sometimes seen as a *process* model of education, whereby the processes in which the child engages are themselves the learning outcome sought. The children benefit from 'doing' because the teacher understands the nature of play and the way in which children structure and use experience. In other schools, although lip service is paid to the concept, the way in which such learning is accomplished is less well understood. Teachers may embrace the principle of learning through doing without actually allowing the child to become a part of the intellectual processes involved; thinking is hardly allowed and rarely extended. One manifestation of this can be seen in schools where the 'art work' conforms to an adult's concept of what children's work ought to look like. The 'doing' is controlled to such a degree that the child's

involvement is, at best, that of a puzzle-solver or, at worst, that of a slave labouring to allow the teacher's concept to be realized in a childlike way.

The following description of one such incident of controlled 'doing' was given me by Joe Maude, a secondary art specialist observing a reception class while a member of a research group investigating design activities under the auspices of the Royal College of Art:

> I was looking after a group of children who were painting pictures of penguins. The six children were faced with newspaper on their table, pots of ready mixed paint, brushes and paper, and they had attired themselves in old shirts of various sizes and colours. Sleeves had to be rolled up out of the way and buttons done up to protect their schoolclothes. It became immediately clear that the pupils knew exactly what to do. My questions about penguins, colour, size were brushed aside as they set about painting with great enthusiasm and confidence. The teacher had given them a demonstration the previous day of what a penguin should look like and how the painting should be done. They all started with a black bridge shape, on top of which they painted a head, the area under the bridge had to be white and they all had yellow beaks, orange feet, stood on a strip of blue and were covered in white splashes of snow. (Maude, 1986)

Another manifestation may be seen in schools where 'structured play' is embraced as an educational principle. In such so-called play the rules and orders of the play are imposed from without, with limitations upon content and form rigidly applied. All play is structured, but in order for it to be classed as play, that structure must be imposed by, or at least embraced by, the person playing and not belong to someone outside the dream. Children engaged in teacher-controlled 'structured play' are often not playing. They may be active and doing, they may be learning, but unless they are free to explore possibilities they are not playing. The value system is imposed by an outside 'other'. This can result in a damping down of feeling, joy and commitment to the task.

Whereas, in tasks which the child recognizes as its own there is a focusing of feeling and an integration of feeling with the activity. The child then owns both the task and the feeling. These feelings belong to the activity and are embedded in its outcome or configuration. In introspective play ends and means, thought and feeling, are united and integrated. When the child works within a valuing system not its own but belonging to a parent or teacher, there cannot be this submission and integration of feeling with task. The feelings are attached to, subsumed or consumed by, an outside 'other' who has taken over responsibility for evaluation. The child works, or does not work, to please or displease an external govenor rather than its own internal notion of nearness of fit to an imagined reality. The skills of making and playing are not then extended but are blunted and stunted by a loss of confidence in the child's own internal notion of how it ought, might, or could be. The locus of evaluation is shifted from inside to another whose motives and criteria of judgement may be obscure.

Designerly play enables the player to be in control of the evaluation of the actions and activities focused upon some feature of the environment which is being explored. It is possible to structure the environment to encourage such play without dictating the content of the play itself. Such a structure is not only possible but necessary if children are to develop their skills of making and playing.

Design education for the early school years can be achieved quite simply by structuring the environment in such a way as to enable children to perfect the skills of making and playing, and then by giving them the freedom to do so. This does not happen by chance. In a design-orientated classroom the teacher arranges the environment so that the children are free to explore ideas. A variety of materials and possibilities are on offer and these are not static. There is a planned programme of experiences within which exploration can happen. These may centre around some project or theme which itself provides a structure or container for the sharing of experience and ideas and for extending the skills of making and playing. But if children have ideas and interests which are outside the theme these are taken up and accommodated. A design-orientated curriculum is one in which the teachers themselves are open to change, to decision-making and to becoming explorers along with their pupils. Children may not make the step from playing into designing in the early years, but the teacher must. Rather than assuming a rigid role, the teacher becomes engaged in a dance-like confrontation with children and their learning.

Towards design education in the early years
Making meaning through interaction with one's environment by ordering and changing that environment is a fundamental attribute of human beings. These meanings encompass both feelings and thought about one's relationship with and within the physical world.

The young child through playing and making does not only perfect manual and manipulative skills. Symbolic representations, imagining what the world might or could be like, planning and executing environmental changes, are a part of thinking from the infant's earliest days. Cognitive and affective development are inseparable from playing, making and ordering — those activities associated with design capacity and awareness. So too is meaning.

Meanings are personal constructs which are embodied in developmental, cultural and individual experiences. They can change and be changed. They may be symbolic, metaphoric, concrete, rational or irrational, conscious or unconscious, or both. The meanings attached to a particular construct depend upon the orientation of the individual towards that construct at that time. Thus, objects and ideas invested with a 'dream potential' through play take on different meanings which have to do with their role in the unfolding drama of play.

When the child extends this play with objects, materials and ideas by removing from them the constraints of the play itself while retaining control over their 'dream potential' the first step from playing into designing is taken. In designing, the play is harnessed to an idea and in the end play may have to be sacrificed to enable one to perfect the idea. In play, the designing occurs as a part of the unfolding drama; there may or may not be a residue or artefact as tangible evidence of the process of playing. In designing, some artefact or system is the sure result of the processes. In young children the divide between the two activities is so tenuous and amorphous that one would be hard-pressed to say for certain 'this is playing' of 'that is designing'. Nor would one wish to do so. The important issue is that the conditions under which play flourishes and is enriched are similar to those which allow, encourage, enrich and stimulate designing. Both require psychological space where inner and outer reality can fuse in the service of the idea.

In introducing 'design' to the early school curriculum it is necessary to recognize it as a fundamental attribute of being human and that, as such, it may, and *should*, already be a part of the curriculum. If it is not — and evidence suggests that in many classrooms children are not allowed to develop the skills of playing and making — then it is the tenor of the curriculum which must be revised and not just a tiny aspect of it. Not only must parents, teachers and others who influence school practice recognize designing as a fundamental human attribute, they must also recognize the conditions under which it develops and flourishes and which enable children to become more, and not less, skilful at it.

Much that happens in school serves to blunt rather than sharpen a child's sense of wonder at how the world works. Much so-called play is

adult – controlled and structured to such a degree that it ceases to fulfil
the necessary conditions of play: the freedom to order the world to one's
own directions; the freedom of choice of action. The locus of evaluation
is shifted to an outside body. The parent, the teacher, the school, the
educational machine and society in general, take away responsibility for
the child's progress in learning. Playing is the only means most children
have to retain autonomy over their own actions. The skills developed in
playing are also the skills of designing.

References
Baynes, K. (1985), 'A design dimension of the curriculum', conference paper.
    Summer school, Roehampton Institute.

Board of Education (1931), *Report of the Consultative Committee on the Primary
    School* (Hadow Report). London: HMSO.

————————————— (1933), *Infant and Nursery Schools* (Hadow Report).
    London: HMSO.

Central Advisory Council for Education (1967), *Children and Their Primary
    Schools* (Plowden Report). London: HMSO.

Coghill, V. (1987), 'Making meaning through designerly play', unpublished
    PhD thesis. Royal College of Art, London.

Crowe, B. (1983), *Play is a Feeling*. London: Unwin Paperbacks.

Einon, D. (1985), *Creative Play*. New York: Viking Press.

Garvey, C. (1977), *Play*. London: Fontana.

Gombrich, E.H. (1979), *The Sense of Order*. Oxford: Phaidon.

Huizinga, J. (1985), *Homo Ludens: a study of the play element in culture*. London:
    Routledge.

Isaacs, S. (1930), *Intellectual Growth in Young Children*. London: Routledge.

Lethaby, W.R. (1929), *The Encyclopaedia and Dictionary of Education*.
    London: Pitman.

Maude, J. (1986), 'Controlled doing', unpublished MA seminar paper. Royal
    College of Art, London.

Winnicott, D.W. (1958), *Through Paediatrics to Psychoanalysis: collected papers*. London: Tavistock.

——————— (1971), *Playing and Reality*. London: Tavistock.

Wells, G. (ed.) (1983), *Learning Through Interaction: the study of language development*. Cambridge: Cambridge University Press.

Willes, M.J. (1983), *Children into Pupils*. London: Routledge.

Chapter Five
The Basis of Designerly Thinking in Young Children
Ken Baynes

It is now five years since the Design Council set up a working party to look at the role of 'design-related activities' in primary schools. This was a significant step in the development of design education because, until then, it had very much been centred in the secondary school. Design education, in fact, has emerged upside down. A design A-level was introduced by the Oxford Board in the late 1960s and the familiar form of design faculty combining (amongst others) art and design, craft, design and technology, and home economics, was first seen in Leicestershire comprehensives at the same time. It would almost certainly have been better to start the other way round by investigating and understanding the roots of design ability as seen in the behaviour of young children. This process is just beginning and it is my aim to set out something of what we know.

It is typical of all human societies, however basic their culture and technology, that they create a made world from the natural resources in the environment. Everywhere groups of people have made shelters, settlements, tools and utensils. The work of doing this is as much a part of the definition of 'human-ness' as the use of language, living together in ordered social groups, or the attempt to explain philosophically what life is about. It is characteristic of people that they not only adapt to the world in which they live, they change it. This is one of the things that accounts for the remarkable success of human beings as a species. But *how* do they do it? What mental processes, what forms of thinking and feeling, make this possible? It happens that recent work on perception, cognitive psychology and psychoanalysis provides some very helpful explanations.

At the centre of this ability to change the environment is something far more specific: a mental faculty that designing shares with politics and other 'planning ahead' activities. This is the capacity to imagine that the world might be other than the way it is. It is something we take so much for granted that we hardly notice how remarkable it is. This capacity to imagine enables us to sit in an armchair on a winter evening and make plans for the way the garden will look in the summer. It enables town planners to look into the future and see the possibility of a new community coming into being on a carefully chosen site. And it shapes next year's fashions.

Seen in this light, design is the ability to imagine and then bring about desired changes in places, products and communications. How does this kind of imagination work? Recent psychological research suggests that it depends on the ability to form in the mind a complex and realistic model of external reality or imagined things. This model can't be expressed in words. It has parallel properties to the physical world as interpreted through our senses of sight, hearing, touch and taste, and has in fact been shaped by perception.

★   ★   ★

We need to experiment in order to bring the concept alive. Over the last two years, I have played a series of games with teachers that aim to reveal something of its nature. They use the cognitive modelling ability and help to make clear what a remarkable aspect of thought it is. Here they are:

1. Imagine that the room we are in is entirely purple.
   Ask these questions:
   Did you imagine it to be one colour purple or various tones and shades of purple?
   Did you like it?
   Did you imagine that the people in the room were purple too?

2. Cast your mind back to childhood. Remember in 'the mind's eye' either a place that you disliked or one that you liked. Write down a brief description of it.

   Typical memories are of the mysterious place 'under granny's stairs', of the sunlit seaside, or the terror of a dentist's surgery.
   Ask these questions:
   How did the memory come to you?
   Did you feel the sun?

Were you able to recall the smell of the dentist's room?
Could you hear sounds as well as see sights?

3. Imagine a cup and saucer. In the mind, pick up a teaspoon and hit the side of the cup with it. Then balance the spoon across the top of the cup.
   Ask these questions:
   What kind of cup did you imagine? (People imagine or model a particular cup, not a generalized one).
   Was there tea in the cup?
   Which way up did you balance the spoon?
   Did you hear a sound when you hit the cup?

5. Imagine we are in a spaceship escaping from a world that is about to be totally destroyed by deadly meteorites.
   Ask these questions:
   What emotions do you feel?
   What kind of an interior are we in?
   What can you see through the imagined windows of your imagined spaceship?
   Is there a noise?
   In the imagined scene are you inside the spaceship or are you 'outside' it, looking on as you might at a scene in a film? (Both are common forms of modelled reality.)

What is extraordinary is not so much the fascinating variety of what people can say about what they imagine, but that they can imagine at all. The perceptual and conceptual power of the ability should not be under-estimated. It is the mental capacity that enables people to handle and have access to environmental experiences that they have had in the past and to project new ideas into the future.

★   ★   ★

So far all of this is in the mind. But human beings have taken a further step that makes it possible for them to share their imaginings with each other. They have created external equivalents for these internal models. Again, these are familiar things: drawings, plans, mathematical symbols, books, prototypes, computer programmes. They are the media through which 'designery thinking' moves from the personal world of the mind into the shared world of social discussion and action.

These external equivalents make it possible to organize the social effort necessary to build or make something because they 'make visible' — allow us to see — the character of what is proposed. Without them, the cognitive models would remain the private property of those that imagine them, fascinating and entertaining perhaps, but socially dumb, unable to inspire the collective effort necessary to bring them to fruition.

It is evident that these cognitive models are at the apex of people's perceptual transactions with the outside world. We know that such transactions can only have certain contents. We cannot perceive *everything* that is out there because our senses are only capable of a relatively narrow band of data. There are sound waves which we cannot hear; light waves we cannot see. Beyond this strict physical limitation, other limitations come from the process by which we learn to perceive the world. It seems clear that this is not a passive receiving. It is an active process in which each growing individual 'selects', actually seeks out, a personal register from the chaos of incoming sense data. We do it partly by acting on the world to create new information for ourselves. From the start our relationship with the world is speculative and experimental.

Ever since the Gastalt psychologists introduced the idea that children have an in-built pattern of intelligence that predisposes them to recognize qualities such as proximity, sameness, closure, symmetry and contrast, we have caught more and more glimpses of the 'lexicon' or grammar that human beings use in their perceptual transactions with the physical world. We know now that even very young babies have well-formed and usable concepts of objects and the edges of objects and of the difference between solids and voids. They react to these in intelligent and self-preserving ways. Evidently the brain's ability to sort out these physical phenomena into a meaningful pattern is active a long time before the ability to name them.

Further evidence of the Gestalt view can be found in what people have actually made. There is a clear and direct link between the perceptual predisposition and the design output of human societies. Here again proximity, sameness, closure, symmetry and contrast (amongst others) are qualities that can be seen in buildings and products from all cultures. Rather as with the world's languages which are hugely varied but which all display the underlying logic and form of language, so too with designs. Designed things exist in extraordinary variety but all exhibit the underlying logic and form of the made. We would never, for example, mistake a made object for a natural structure. So finely tuned is our design intelligence that it could never make such a mistake, any more than our linguistic intelligence could mistake birdsong for a poem even though exactly the same senses are involved. On the other hand, our brilliance at handling and interpreting cognitive models enables us to recognize the connection between the two and weave them into metaphors of great subtlety.

In his book *Frames of Mind*, Howard Gardner (1984) discusses the idea of 'multiple intelligence'. He describes the growing biological evidence for locating certain kinds of thinking and feeling in particular parts of the brain. Although it is clear that the brain has extraordinary recuperative powers and that it can shift functions around to circumvent damage, it is also clear that this work of substitution has rather strict limits. There is a physical developmental process called 'canalization' which has the effect of confirming and crystallizing paths of use and custom in and between the different areas of the brain. It is rather as if a highway were to be made wider and its route more fixed directly by the passage and amount of the traffic using it. After a certain point, different for different functions, the route becomes permanent and cannot be changed or replaced.

Gardner argues that with this new biological understanding goes a change of philosophical approach. In the immediate past, the common view has been that all 'intelligence' is really the same thing — a particular style of thinking and reasoning which we apply to widely differing activities. We can see that this idea has had a powerful influence in education where, for example, problem-solving has been identified as a fundamental human strategy discoverable in every school subject. But with the strong physical location of different functions there has developed the concept that different kinds of intelligence actually depend on the existence of distinctive kinds of mental processes. Gardner is quite clear, for example, that spatial intelligence involves its own perceptions, depends on its own 'language' and is expressed in very particular behaviour. It also relates to a particular side of the brain.

If I were to attempt to characterize 'design intelligence' in this way, I would argue that:

1. it is speculative, directed towards imagining changes in the environment;
2. it exists because cognitive modelling makes it possible to form an internal 'representation' of imagined changes;
3. it exists socially because externalized physical models can form an

external 'representation' of imagined changes — these are its language, the medium through which it finds shared expression that leads to social action; and

4. its content is determined by the 'rules' of human perception and these perceptual boundaries are vividly re-expressed, perhaps reinforced, in the environmental change that people imagine and the environments they create.

*   *   *

When dealing with any aspect of human intelligence it is useful for teachers to be able to distinguish between the inevitable development of an ability and what can be done deliberately and consciously to aid its growth. The analogy between language and design is useful once again. Any baby growing up in an environment where people are talking will learn the use of language. As Noam Chomsky (1968) puts it, humans have a 'language acquisition device'. Language is 'wired in' to the human mind; people are predisposed to learn to speak. As we have seen, recent work on perception and child behaviour shows that babies learn to react intelligently to the world of objects and space even before they can speak. What is more, they very soon take pleasure in making the environment react to their wishes. They do this not only for survival but also in a spirit of playfulness, by themselves and with other people. Humans have a 'wired-in' predisposition to explore and change their environment. In the case of language, however, it is well understood that this development process will fall far short of human potential if it is not deliberately fostered by education. For the rudimentary language acquisition device to grow into an effective and *consciously available* tool for thought and social discourse it requires the mutual exchange of learning and teaching. Without this, human beings will remain alienated from an unrealized part of themselves and, further, be cut off from the ideas and insights of others, now and in the past.

Exactly the same is true of the wired-in predisposition to interpret and shape the environment. Unless it is deliberately fostered through teaching and learning, access to it will be lost by those who once possessed it. They will grow up dumb in this respect, unable to communicate effectively with themselves or other people about this aspect of human behaviour. To some degree this has been well understood by parents and teachers. The almost universal existence of toys demonstrates one of the ways in which different cultures have encouraged small children to engage in play with objects. In the home, mothers seem always to have invited children to join in domestic, environmental work and have done this not only as a necessity but as a vivid kind of informal education.

Psychoanalysts have provided a further interpretation of this nurturing that identifies the mother as the child's first environment. A purposeful awareness of her geography — and by analogy other geographies — comes from this first interactive relationship with a world separate from the self. The elements of time, space and physical form (fundamental to all design work) are, in the mother's body, brought vividly alive in the cycle of hunger and its satisfaction.

Vera Coghill (1987; see pp.56-69 above), a nursery school teacher and designer who has been studying the design ability of very young children, has seized on the significance of Winnicott's work on the 'transitional object'. She recognizes, in his analysis of the particular attachment of a child to a beloved thing, the emergence of that special sensibility towards the environment that enables people to create places and products that combine symbolic and practical utility in a single entity. From this modest beginning in a magical shawl or teddy, it expands into the extraordinary mass of manipulatable resources that fill the cupboards and cover the floors of nurseries in the industrialized world. Here is a highly visible portion of the raw materials with which the three-year old's design capacity does its work!

It is significant that both Pestalozzi and Froebel saw in caring mothers the best model for the primary school teachers of the future. Froebel's 'mothering made conscious' was partly based on his observations of the way in which peasant mothers drew children into the world of their work and encouraged them to learn through this experience. The provision of a rich learning environment at school was emphasized by Froebel who also called for 'light, airy, classrooms'. This pioneer thinking gradually became accepted so that as early as the 1870s there were kindergartens inspired by these ideas established in working-class districts. By the 1890s the approach was adopted as official policy by the Board of Education. Before the First World War Rachel and Margaret McMillan set up garden and camp schools in south-east London where the child's curiosity about the physical world was given a central place in the pedagogical strategy. Between the wars ordinary practice absorbed more and more of the 'modern' ethos. And after the Second World War, primary schools were deliberately designed with windows on the outside world and made full of learning materials to do with 'proximity, sameness, closure, symmetry and contrast'.

Why, then, does it now seem necessary to do more? Partly because these pioneers emphasized playing with the environment for its own sake. In accepting the importance of physical, tactile, sensual development they seem to have forgottten that shaping the environment is an active cognitive process in which reason and speculation are also involved. It is as though these pioneers were teaching half of an experience, encouraging children to listen to sounds and to make sounds, but not to turn the sounds into words to create stories, poems or songs. The children encountered the world of objects, they played with and drew and modelled natural things, they handled clay, sand and water (and sometimes even fire), but they were not asked to use their experience to make a world of their own. They were not shown that people everywhere had used exactly these resources to bring about changes in places, products and communications, and that they could do the same.

★   ★   ★

Design is about the future. It is also about working in society. If the main drive of the artist is to realize for him or herself the *inner* world of the imagination, the job of the designer is to do this for other people in the *outer* world of the environment. How do other people want to live? How can I help them achieve it? These are the design questions.

It may be that Piaget's influence has helped to keep these designerly questions out of the primary classroom. When discussing young children in this context, we are confronted by work that seems to demonstrate the essential self-centredness of their perceptual experience. Piaget himself suggested that pre-school children are incapable of imagining viewpoints other than their own. He tried to show that they have an understanding of time that is like a relatively unconnected series of film stills. However, Margaret Donaldson (1978) has challenged Piaget very directly in her book *Children's Minds*. She says that provided the social setting makes sense to them, children of this age can in fact 'de-centre' effectively and so can imagine the situations and experience of other people. For design education this is a crucial issue: to have design experience it is essential to imagine alternative worlds and to foresee the possibility of change taking place through time.

There is considerable evidence that even very small children achieve 'designerly' de-centring in their play. If we watch children playing free from the inhibitions of toys that adults have provided, or the formalities of organized play, what we often see is a very special interaction

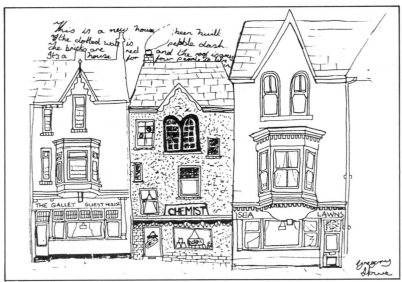

Figures 5.1 to 5.4:
Work by Welsh
primary school
children that
involved close
observation and
critical analysis of
existing buildings
and making
proposals for a new
building to fill a
gap in the High
Street (Art and the
Built Environment
project:
Cwmrhydyceirw
and Ynstawe
Primary Schools,
West Glamorgan)

between things and the imagination. One group of teachers working on design awareness at the Royal College of Art came up with a very simple and evocative general description of this kind of play. They called it 'role playing with props'. This beautifully describes the little boy who all alone and absorbed pushes pieces of stick up and down a pile of gravel while making sounds of a heavy lorry. But it also captures the essence of the group of little girls who arrange their dolls and teddies on the lawn for tea in front of sycamore leaf plates with bacon and eggs made of yellow nasturtium flowers and strips of pink paper. While doing these things they are absorbed in an imaginative re-creation of elsewhere. It is certain that they have de-centred into an imagined space.

Piaget placed such importance on the scientific, rational mode of thought that he put it at the pinnacle of his model of the child's development. His books are really a study of the way in which this particular 'frame of mind' emerges and becomes available to the child. Inevitably, other frames of mind appear in a rather distorted form when viewed through this teleological telescope. In his fascinating discussion of the child's developing understanding of the environment, Piaget concentrates on the growth of scientific analysis and not on the ability to shape the environment or imagine the existence of alternative environments. It will be important to re-work Piaget's environmental observations to give proper weight to this 'shaping' aspect of the child's intelligence.

In our own work on the Schools Council 'Art and the Built Environment'[1] project, we became convinced that even six- and seven-year olds could make realistic and enlightening critical judgements about towns and buildings and that they could de-centre sufficiently to engage in design activity. Older children, of course, brought more experience and hence more subtlety to this activity. What the teacher needed to do was to direct attention to the 'designerly' aspects of the world and then introduce the most suitable media for study. 'Media' here means both the social media of learning and the physical media of learning: drawings, words or photographs.

I should like to include here an extended extract from a paper I gave in 1982 at the Open University. It describes a typical sequence of 'Art

---

[1] This project was based first at the Town and Country Planning Association (1976-80), then at the Royal College of Art (1980-83). In the first phase it was directed by Colin Ward with Eileen Adams as its field officer; in the second phase it was co-directed by Eileen Adams and Ken Baynes. (Adams, 1982; Adams and Baynes, 1982; Adams and Ward, 1982)

and the Built Environment' work. It demonstrates an educational approach that has proved to be effective in helping children to realize something of their inherent design intelligence. It is by no means the only way to do it. However, it is one way to do it and it is useful as an example of how the theoretical background can in fact be brought alive in the classroom.

* * *

If cognitive modelling is fundamental to designing and design awareness, how can it find a place in the classroom? What we can say with confidence is that educationally these interior models have to be exteriorized before they can be the subject of analysis, reflection, discussion and further development. The point is that, unless this happens, the teacher cannot know what is going on in his or her children's heads and, probably more vital, the children cannot know what is going on in each other's heads. The uses of drawing and photography in 'Art and the Built Environment' work are all to do with this process of exteriorizing and then studying and manipulating the results.

The approach means that drawings and photographs are seen as conceptual tools and not as an end in themselves. They will always have a definable purpose which can transcend their status and quality as products, though we recognize that quality is an important element in the creation of concepts and the making of meaning. Seen in this context, the use of drawing in the project is, in its humble way, a part of the tradition of objective drawing that has its roots in the Renaissance. This has always concerned itself with a humanistic interpretation of the man-made as well as aiding scientific enquiry and providing designers with their most powerful means of shaping what Herbert Read called 'the forms of things unknown'. What we have found is that all these functions of drawing and photography are available to and understandable by children.

In our use of drawing for its conceptual power there is, however, a proviso. We start from and respect the child's direct and emotive response to real buildings and places. This is the foundation of environmental experience. We would argue that it is only this emotional commitment that can, in the end, provide an adequate motivation for study, for critical judgement and, finally, for the confidence to take responsibility for changing and improving the environment. Here is how a typical cycle of work might develop using drawing and photography as one of a number of means of study leading up to design activity:

What am I experiencing?

First, streetwork, getting out into the most comprehensive and least costly learning resource available. Here you can see, touch, hear, smell the environment. How do you react? What do you like, what do you dislike? Is it exciting, boring, cosy, threatening, enclosed, windy, noisy, quiet, peaceful, colourful? Drawing and photography are used as notes, as aids to memory, to interrupt and capture the stream of perceptions and reactions that come crowding in. They serve to focus attention and, with practice, can help people to see and analyse what might otherwise go unnoticed and certainly unrecorded. Specific study methods can be used to give shape and direction to this 'enquiry' into the nature of the man-made world. The result is a stock of raw material, based on direct experience, and ready for further study and analysis. Characteristically, drawings produced in these conditions are smudgy and battered, unfinished looking, but also immediate and forceful, reeking of hard experience and personal judgement. They tend to be difficult to interpret. They are primarily for the person who did them: reports from the battle to understand and record environmental experience.

Why do I think what I think?

Next, classroom development. This is one of the most difficult stages to explain. It consists of reworking the street material so as to clarify the nature of the direct experience and to make a start on explaining it. It is still personal, but there will be discussions with the teacher and the feeling of common purpose that comes from working in a classroom where other people are engaged in a similar task. A lot of informal learning takes place within the group as people go round to see what everyone else is up to.

Drawings and photography play the major role in making it possible for those taking part to open up and look into their experiences, to 'relive' them, while also attempting to offer an explanation of why they felt what they felt. The existence of images supports and focuses the discussion of environmental experience which is beginning to emerge; it also makes it possible to depict, to recreate in an accessible form, the qualities which have given rise to the personal reactions that are now being analysed by those who experienced them. Drawings made at this stage have a searching, didactic quality. They show evidence of the struggle for understanding and explanation; they are moving out from personal shorthand towards more commonly available styles and idioms.

How can I explain and justify what I think?

Group presentation. The basis of critical judgement, as understood in the project, is the ability to explain to oneself and others why you like or dislike a building or a place, why it is the way it is, what are the ingredients that make it tick as a place. Typically this is explored in a group session in which individuals or small groups make a presentation which is intended to meet this responsibility to explain. It is hard to imagine how this could be done without the repertoire of visual communication: maps, plans, diagrams, models, illustrations, photographs — anything that can offer the basis for qualitative judgement and insight.

What ususally happens is that people mount and then talk about a small exhibition which stands for and represents their reworked, exteriorized, analysed experience. This is followed by discussion, by the putting of alternative views and explanations, by the emergence of a broader picture of the ways in which people can respond to and understand the human meaning of the built environment. At this stage it is the whole presentation that needs to be considered, rather than individual drawings and photographs. Taken together, these now form a graphic statement and each element within the statement will have a defined purpose and message.

How might it be?

Design activity. There is a natural progression from understanding how buildings and places have come to be the way they are, to asking how they might be in the future. Many of the techniques that can be used for exploring the physical reality of the existing environment can be deployed to give substance to proposals for change and improvement. Here drawing and photography take their place with a range of other 'modelling' media to make it possible for groups of children to work together to experience the conflict of requirements that is basic to all designing.

Behind this activity are two interlinked questions: How do people want to live their lives in this place? How might this place be changed to help them to live in the way they want? A great variety of drawings can be helpful in this and their purpose is to make the future possibilities transparent and manipulable at an appropriate level of detail.

Two examples: a rough site plan, quickly drawn, with basic cut-outs for houses, will make it possible for a group to try out and grasp the implications of alternative layouts; recording the layouts with a Polaroid camera will ensure that the alternatives are not forgotten and that one can be compared with another. Descriptive drawings can then be used to give reality to the imagined views from the house windows, so foreseeing the effect of each layout on such things as privacy, isolation, or landscape quality. Here again, drawings and photographs will have a specific purpose: to research, create and make visible the alternatives.

Can I justify my vision of how it might be?
Group presentation. The previous group presentation was to justify and explain responses to the existing environment: this one is to look to the future and the changes it could contain. At the presentation each group takes responsibility for its design proposals and attempts to explain the change of reasoning that led members to their conclusions. The typical medium is, once again, an exhibition which stands for and embodies in concrete form the group's experience, arguments and proposals. Without this focus it would be very difficult indeed to share the experience with others or show them with any degree of realism what has been designed. The presentation invites and makes inevitable a comparison of different views and is, in itself, a learning experience of great power. The various forms of modelling make it possible.

*   *   *

What I have tried to show in this chapter is that design ability and design awareness are inherent in all human beings. People everywhere shape their surroundings in purposeful ways. To do this they use the kinds of mental processes and social organization that I have outlined. Behind the argument, of course, is the idea that schools can and should help foster this aspect of the child's intelligence just as they do language and social skills. I hope it is clear by now that art and design are not in fact the same thing. Design has unique characteristics of its own: for example, its concern with the future and its search for practical answers to human needs. However, it shares many concerns with art teaching and any teacher who sees the value of art in children's development will be likely to understand the broader perspective that design-related activity has to offer.

However important design activity is, it would almost certainly be a mistake to develop it in primary education as a separate subject. One of the strengths of design activity is its cross-curricular nature. Primary teachers will want to build on this: if they do, design work can come to find its place quite naturally as a logical part of the integrated primary school day. If design is treated in this way it will make sense to the children and reinforce and complement the other aspects of their mental and social development.

References

Adams, E. (1982), *Art and the Built Environment: working parties*. York: Longman Resources Unit/Schools' Council.

Adams, E. and Baynes, K. (1982), *Art and the Built Environment: study activities*. York: Longman Resources Unit/Schools' Council.

Adams, E. and Ward, C. (1982), *Art and the Built Environment: a teacher's approach*. Harlow: Longman/Schools' Council.

Coghill, V. (1987), 'Making meaning through designerly play', unpublished PhD thesis. Royal College of Art, London.

Chomsky, N. (1968), *Language and Mind*. New York: Harcourt Brace Jovanovich.

Donaldson, M. (1978), *Children's Minds*. London: Fontana/Collins.

Gardner, H. (1984), *Frames of Mind*. London: Heinemann.

Chapter Six
Direct Sensory Experience as the Source of Nourishment for Ideas, Concepts and Imagination
Keith Gentle

As a child I always remembered, rather vaguely, perhaps as in a dream, a beautiful box of bricks. The patterns I could weave and build with these were, to me, magical. At some time, though, this box of bricks had been put away.

One day I found them in the attic where my father had stored them along with other 'discarded' toys and the general accumulations of families. My excitement at re-discovering them was immense.

Years later, when I smell that peculiar mixture of dust, polish and old, faded newspapers which seems to hang about attics, I recall vividly not just the attic but the deep sense of pleasure and satisfaction from building and making patterns with bricks.

We can all recall similar personal memories from our own childhood, either in moments of quiet reflection or, more especially, when they are triggered off by some catalyst, such as a sound, smell, taste or situation. These 'triggered' reflections of earlier experience reveal something of the power and penetration into the psyche of early, direct experience. That these moments should have such long-lasting traces is remarkable: perhaps we should recognize their significance more clearly in education as being formative and important stimuli.

Direct, sensory experience comes about when we become involved in handling and enjoying contact with things. It includes the awakening of one or more of our senses which can trigger other sensations: sight, awareness of space and place, motion and relationship (the kinaesthetic sense), sound and touch, taste and smell, all of which act as sensors of the world around us. As well as being sensors, our senses can be seen as 'windows' into our own inner state, into our awareness, sensory and perceptual understanding, and general well-being.

It seems that where direct sensory experience occurs there is a peculiar and highly personal selection or focusing taking place at the initial moment of response. This focusing also seems to attract particular energies, both sensitive and reflective. It is almost as though one is arrested by the sensation and has to draw as much from it as possible, whether through recalling the association and context of the experience or just savouring it. Such deeply personal experiences can be likened to receiving 'nourishment', similar to the experience of being nourished by food.

Sensory experiences do seem to nourish mental, emotional and imaginative growth, as can be seen, for example, in the connections and relationships, the sense of well-being and satisfaction, the ideas and concepts, which arise as a result: as Daniel Stern (1977) points out, 'infants, from birth, will seek out sensory stimulation and even work for it. Such seeking for stimulation achieves the same status as a drive — such as hunger'. Stern further states that such 'stimulation is needed to provide the brain with the "raw materials" required for the maturation of perceptual, cognitive and sensori-motor processes' (ibid.). In other words, we need sensory stimulation which, if taken from us, can be deeply disturbing for our health and well-being.

One of the most cruel forms of torture is that of deprivation of one, several, or all of the senses. Disorientation can result, even to the point of loss of sense of self or identity. This shows that sensory experiences, which we can take for granted or overlook, enable us to establish and maintain aspects of identity and to renew and sustain them; in very young children this is clearly crucial in their formative years.

Sensory experience keys us into the appearance and behaviours, the relationships and structure, and the changing states of objects, places, people and environments in the world around us (see Figure 6.1). Such qualities as the weight, texture, solidity, softness, flavour, scent, taste and tone of the environment are felt in this way; or the closeness or remoteness, scale and density, distance and level of an encounter, whether this is with an object, plant, person or place. All these experiences create the background understanding of the world around.

In order to develop an intelligence about any aspect of our environment, we need to 'play' with, to explore, to investigate or analyse its qualities or properties. This process of discovering and coming to terms with new experience can form a short or long part of familiarization. As adults we have to realize how much of our experience is vicarious, partial, or interpreted through similar or

Figure 6.1: Playing on the beach

parallel experiences. The fresh directness and spontaneity of children is something we can admire but not easily emulate; the patterns of our minds are too well formed.

★   ★   ★

The forming of patterns of understanding in the mind starts from the earliest interactions with the environment. Young children need to 'control' or 'order' their experiences if they are to survive the increasingly complex influx of sensations. Margaret Donaldson (1978) quotes the work of Papousek, who argues that babies try to achieve control over stimuli and in doing so match 'incoming information about the world against some sort of inner standard'. She suggests that this amounts to saying that the babies are already engaged in building some kind of 'model' of bits of the world, some mental representation of what it is like.

We all need such 'models' in order to orientate ourselves to new experiences, to cope with changes and developments, and to maintain stability and confidence in our ordinary relationships. At different times in our development such pattern formation takes new and radically different forms. In infancy much of a child's experience is immediate and direct. New learning has to be in the context of the child's experience and not abstracted from it, if it is to register and be intelligible. Learning is centred on self, but not limited *by* self, where the child's understanding fits appropriately new patterns of interaction. Thus, as Margaret Donaldson points out, 'young children make sense of what people do when they talk and act rather than by what their words mean. The child's interpretation of words is strongly influenced by his own independent structuring of the context' (ibid.).

Throughout infancy the structuring of experience becomes more complex and developed, although still self-centred. Approaching seven years old, the way in which children understand the world, and structure their experience of it, changes significantly. They begin to understand differences and similarities, to understand objects from different points of view, and to realize that the same object can appear different from different vantage points. They develop concepts from which to structure their understanding of the world.

Children's experience expands enormously as they build concepts. The building of concepts enables them to explain and negotiate, share and collaborate, play games and make up rules. Their questions and investigations lead to a considerable expansion of their known world; their interest is in finding out how things work, what they mean, how they are put together, and so on. In order to manage this shift in viewpoint and understanding, children become increasingly dependent on their own imagined view of how the world works, adding to and modifying this view with experience. Imaginative ideas are used to scale down the real world to manageable proportions and interpret it in ways that enable the child to cope with an expanding reality.

We all develop and use our own ideas, or assimilate the ideas of others, in order to make our experience of the world intelligible and manageable. It is about the age of seven, when children develop self-awareness, that this way of thinking and understanding emerges and their play becomes more inventive.

Inventiveness is a significant attribute of human intelligence and behaviour. Inventiveness works with ideas, building on to or adapting, assembling or remaking objects, materials or processes to fulfil some new function or purpose. It also has another significant dimension which is more to do with the individual and the development of his or her own self than with the objects and materials around them. After seven years old, children will sense and understand what it is to be 'grown up' and invent various games and personal idiosyncratic strategies to help them achieve the 'status' of grown-ups on their own terms. As Bettelheim says:

> Just because his life is often bewildering to him, the child needs even more to be given the chance to understand himself in this complex world with which he must learn to cope. He needs ideas on how to bring his inner house into order and on that basis to create order in his life. (Bettelheim, 1977)

Much of the inventiveness characteristic of this period (from seven years onwards) is motivated by the increased awareness of self in relation to the world of adults; how they behave, what excites and interests them, and how adults manage the world over which they seem to have such command. The shift in understanding which comes about through the capacity to build concepts places a premium on personal ideas, as Schumacher recognized. He wrote:

> When we think, we think with ideas. Our mind is not just a blank, a tabula rasa. When we begin to think we can begin to do so only because our mind is already filled with all sorts of ideas with which to think. (Schumacher, 1974)

He goes on to make an important reference from this viewpoint, which is pertinent to the present argument:

> If the mind cannot bring to the world a set, or shall we say a tool-box, of powerful ideas, the world must appear to it as a chaos, a mass of unrelated phenomena, of meaningless events. (ibid.)

This, then, is the deeper significance of children's own ideas. They are the essential means whereby they make sense and personal order out of their experience of the world, however this experience is provided. I believe that using personal ideas to interpret and understand experience is a natural process which leads to individual growth. Opportunities may affect the range and extent of such growth but it is for us as teachers to see the significance for it of personal ideas.

*   *   *

Reflection on our own experience and the quiet observation of children and young people, will reveal other signs of the importance and function of ideas. Three examples can be cited.

Firstly, there seems to be greater motivation where personal ideas are in force. It is as though the purpose of an endeavour comes into sharper focus and the reasons for it do not have to be questioned or examined. The work in hand has its own momentum and becomes self-evidently necessary. In some cases the tasks undertaken, which arise from a child's own ideas, seem fantastic and impossible yet they are pursued to the point of frustration because the idea seemed good. Children's ideas are often very different from the safe, carefully structured, things which teachers might encourage.

Secondly, the quality of attention, the focusing of energy, thought and imagination on the task in hand, seems heightened. The set of the shoulders, the facial expression and the look in the eyes all tell us that the activity is deeper than a surface response and is making other connections than those asked for or supposed by the teacher. Such attention may last for only a short time but can be longer if the climate in which children learn is conducive to concentration. Too often it can be the teacher's noise and interruptions which inhibit such personal learning.

Thirdly, ideas seem to personalize the learning that is taking place. Often children will restate what they have been told or shown in their own way, as if to make it more definitely theirs. Sometimes they will make lateral references to, or analogies with, other experience, showing that the 'frame or reference' they are using to understand something is different from that of the teacher. This personalizing of learning seems to be an essential way in which the mind works, dealing in its own pattern of understanding and inner imagery to interpret and accommodate new learning.

I believe that all these aspects of learning are crucial to any understanding of children's inventiveness. Furthermore, insight into how children's ideas are stimulated and how they learn from them is, in my view, essential to an understanding of how children relate to problem-solving and design experience. Designing, in one important way, can be seen as the act of sorting something out so that it makes sense and works for you. This 'sorting out' may or may not involve specific objective functions but, for children especially, it just makes something more comfortable to be with, or more manageable. For example, the effort involved in arranging objects or planning games, or the energy put into playing with materials, can be designing in this sense. Shapes and patterns are evolved only to be changed and remade as ideas change and evolve.

*   *   *

These comments indicate that an important function of children's ideas is to interpret and find personal meaning in experience, and this is a necessary way in which the human mind learns. Too often the value of making and doing in children's learning in primary schools seems to be in results which the teacher has engineered (sometimes literally): work in art, craft and design seems to be a teacher-organized and teacher-directed activity. Almost invariably, the things children are asked to do have to fit into a theme or project or, alternatively, the teacher has a technique or end-product in mind which the children's work must match.

Thus, the things which children are expected to do which might come into the category of art, craft or design, are reduced to simple, technique-based, or copied, stereotypes which have little personal meaning for them. The significant elements which are missing are exactly those which arise from children's genuine, inventive behaviour, namely, personal motivation, the focusing of attention and individual meaning.

Children are so used to meanings and purposes being given to the things they do, and to words being used to express these purposes, that it is difficult to register personal meanings in other ways. Words are too readily used to stand for experiences in this context, so that it is easy to forget that much of our understanding comes about in a quite different way: it comes about through our direct action. This is particularly the case with children who do not readily abstract understandings from what they just see and hear. They need to develop a rich pattern of practical experiences and interactions with people, things and materials for this to happen.

Brenda Crowe writes:

> Words are only worth as much as personal experience has made them mean. Without meaning words are useless but, as I found everywhere, experience without words can have both power and meaning at a deep level of knowing. (Crowe, 1983)

Such knowing, then, can derive from handling objects, materials and living things; from being in a variety of different environments and situations; and from participating or sharing imaginatively in the creative experiences of others.

*   *   *

There are certain kinds of intelligence about the world which grow directly from action and from sensory experience. For example, our tactile, spatial or visual intelligence about how phenomena behave or physical aspects relate together arise from our direct experience of them. As Thomas Blakeslee writes:

> In this word orientated world, it is easy to overlook the fact that we have many other kinds of thought besides verbal thought. Thinking, after all, consists of the manipulation and re-arrangement of memory images. The ultimate source of the memory images used in thought is our senses. Since vision is the most information-rich of the senses, visual thinking is extremely important and powerful. (Blakeslee, 1980)

If we consider the kinds of experience which are associated with one aspect of our senses it is possible to see how a particular kind of intelligence about the world might be developed or neglected. Blakeslee goes as far as to say:

> When we think verbally we are limited by the constraints of our verbal memory. Verbal meaning is largely determined by the order in which words occur. (ibid.)

In relation to art, craft and design it is interesting and appropriate to look at the kind of intelligence which arises from experiences which develop our kinaesthetic sense, that sense to do with space, location and movement. For example, such experiences as moving up, into, between, over, on top of, beneath and through. All these relate us spatially and through motion to our immediate environment. Judgement of speed, distance, scale, position and size are similarly related to our kinaesthetic sense. The capacity to inhabit environments imaginatively, or to identify with other physical situations than our own, arises from such kinaesthetic, sensory experience.

When we are conscious of our own kinaesthetic sense working we can but marvel at it. For example, when driving a car we not only maintain the momentum, road position and relationship to other vehicles, but are also able to feel accurately where the switches and levers are that we need in order to do so. At night when we drive this special sense is even more apparent when we seem to be able to judge accurately the distance and exact position of a switch. This sense is made more facile and fluent through repetition and practice, but does seem to depend on a very acute awareness of our position in relation to many other things around us. One could say with driving, as with many other things in our lives, that we develop an intelligent sense of where we are and how we need to act.

★   ★   ★

It is this kind of *intelligent sensing* that I wish to bring into focus in this chapter, as it is something which we need to develop very early in our lives. It seems to me that one sees the beginnings of this intelligent sensing when watching young babies exploring their environment and finding out how to negotiate themselves around it. Intelligent sensing is also evident in much of the playing and making behaviour of children: such activity as building on previous experience with intelligent guesswork, coping with mistakes, adapting ideas and materials to new uses and inventing solutions to problems. Play is often the motivation and context for such learning as it is never too risky and always successful in the child's terms through being readily adapted or changed.

Does the need to design arise from sensing needs in this kind of way? For example, sensing the need for some kind of action, reorganization, rethinking or adaptation of some object of environment? Firstly, one assumes that there must be some feeling that there is a 'problem', a disjunction, lack of connection or function which requires personal thought, response or action. Thus prompted, the mind can skim round the store-house of experiences, knowledge and understandings to come up with an idea that might resolve the perceived problem.

In this way, sensing a problem should come before seeking its solution. In education, it is often someone else's problem which is expected to become an intriguing and stimulating way of learning. One could say, of course, that if no problems were posed by the teacher, the whole area of learning through problem-solving may never arise in a child's experience. In my view, however, such a notion is challenged by the facts of children's learning and playing. The question arises as to how much this sensing a problem is an automatic, natural response and how much it has been or has to be cultivated. Although the original meaning of the term 'to design' was 'to draw', over recent decades it has taken on a broader meaning associated with planning, thinking out, devising ways and shaping alternatives. In children's play, these activities can be seen continually, growing out of action and being stimulated by it.

It is by doing things that children reveal, or sense, needs as well as come to ways of sorting them out. Some of these needs (or, in design terms, problems) will become apparent in the handling of materials; others will be revealed in playing with or sharing objects; or again, imaginative play will promote the need to make or invent something to extend or satisfy an imaginative idea. I remember one of my own children using boxes of all kinds in a variety of ways to create environments and living quarters for an Action Man toy. Cutting, bending, sticking and joining were all motivated by the need to make things for Action Man, from a writing desk with drawers to a geometry set, all to scale.

Sometimes the problems are technical and require the help of an adult to show the right direction or point to a source of information. This was the case with a child who wanted to light a Lego house. The adult has to be wary of taking the initiative for the work and negating the child's own ideas and motivation. Even when this is in danger of happening, children will find ways of making it their own.

Children's confidence in their own ideas and ways of finding things out diminish where the views and knowledge of an adult become too dominant, especially in a teaching situation. If the pattern of relationships between teacher and taught is one in which the teacher dominates and tends towards directing the children's work, then the children will be less likely to offer their views or ask their own questions.

Teachers sometimes say that children have no ideas, and when left to their own devices do not know what to do. This may appear to be the case, but one has to question the purposes of teaching, beyond achieving superficial results, and to ask why this situation should arise. Contained within the experience of the things children make are all those important processes which occur between conceiving an idea and giving it form. Such things as bringing together materials and ideas, choosing and rejecting, seeing and trying out possibilities, overcoming frustrations and working through difficulties on the way to achieving results, are an embodiment of such processes as well as a platform from which to take the next step.

★ ★ ★

The teacher's main responsibilty is to see that these processes are stimulated and promoted in the child's education, not to supplement them with short cuts, easy tricks or ready-made answers. It is only when the teacher is open to children's ideas that real design experience, in the way I have described it, can begin. The teacher can stimulate the discussion of ideas in various ways in order to set in motion the exchange of experiences, questions, observations and responses. Giving children first-hand experiences of real things is one important way. That is, experience of real places, of people 'from outside' school, of living things, plants, creatures, objects, some with curiosity or historical interest, others that are everyday or precious. These experiences are very likely to promote discussion and questioning. It is important to create the right atmosphere in which children are going to feel confident to commit themselves to their own points of view, to observations and personal ideas. The idea of creating the right atmosphere is dealt with more fully elsewhere (Gentle, 1985), but it is clearly most important for the development of inventive activity where other kinds of stimuli can be provided. For example, looking at, and, where practicable, taking apart everyday objects, toys or simple mechanisms; proposing uses or alternatives for them; creating environments and habitats; telling stories about them; and so on. Carefully selected scrap materials, unit materials (Lego, wood blocks), clay and wire could, for instance, be used to develop or interpret ideas.

Children's inventiveness and their capacity to create may exist in many different forms and take different directions. Each one can learn from others through the way practices, discoveries and ideas are shared.

Figure 6.2: Vehicle building and testing

The act of sharing discoveries and results with others is as important a part of learning as the direct collaboration over the same piece of work. Considerable learning from others takes place at primary school age, anyway.

The teaching skills appropriate to intelligent sensing (designing) and making are as much to do with children and teacher learning from each other as directing or proposing ways of working. In fact, open, exploratory attitudes towards making and designing are likely to encourage intelligent sensing from which the motivation to seek personal solutions will grow (see Figure 6.2).

Thus, the main contention of this chapter is that through observing and respecting the learning and playing activity of children in primary school we can see how to develop their intelligent sensing of the world around and the problems and possibilities this reveals. The teacher's interaction with this intelligent sensing and the inventive behaviour it promotes should form the basis of design activity in primary schools and should not be subverted by artificially-posed problems to be solved in the teacher's way and on the teacher's terms.

References

Bettelheim, B. (1977), *The Uses of Enchantment*. New York: Vintage Books.

Blakeslee, T.R. (1980), *The Right Brain*. London: Papermac (Macmillan).

Crowe, B. (1983), *Play is a Feeling*. London: Unwin Paperbacks.

Donaldson, M. (1978), *Children's Minds*, London: Fontana.

Gentle, K. (1985), *Children and Art Teaching*. London: Croom Helm.

Schumacher, E.F. (1974), *Small is Beautiful*. Tunbridge Wells: Abacus.

Stern, D. (1977), *The First Relationship: infant and mother*. London: Fontana.

Chapter Seven
The Role of Humour in Children's Drawing Experience
Sheila Paine

On the day following the first flight of Concorde, I stood in an infant school classroom, overlooking one of the children as he drew. The unique new supersonic passenger aircraft had made its debut on our television screens the previous day for all of thirty seconds as it sprang off the runway and climbed sharply into the sky. In about the same brief period of time as he had taken to observe it and as I watched, the boy created a drawing of the aircraft in its 'take-off' position, undercarriage still extended and protective cockpit 'nose' still lowered for maximum pilot visibility during take-off.

His drawing was not just a schematic portrayal of any aircraft; it was clearly of this new and intriguing aerial machine. In half a minute he had been able to grasp its essential characteristics, in particular its extraordinary resemblance, in beak, wing and claw, to a wild bird. The drawing portrayed a hybrid, both creature and artefact. But it also had a third characteristic: it was funny; the flying creature had an anthropomorphic aspect with a near-human expression and posture.

Such an ability to strike at the heart of observations through drawing is by no means uncommon in the youngest of schoolchildren, as we know, when lack of drawing experience is more than compensated by an as yet uninhibited daring to describe and to comment. It is curious, though, that while early visually descriptive skill in drawing is respected as enterprising achievement, the parallel and complementary facility to draw with expressive humour is frequently regarded as naive accident. I do not refer only to the capacity for the portrayal of funny anecdotes, but also to that mode of drawing referred to by Clive Bell (1934) as 'a purely visual comedy — about forms told in forms — which could be told in no other way'.

Western European social attitudes to humour in art are generally ambivalent anyway, so that the significance of comic expression for the developing individual is largely ignored, just as there seems to be a general reluctance to accept humour as a legitimate ingredient in contemporary art. For some, the wit contained in Picasso's sketchbooks is acceptable only because of his stature as an otherwise serious artist. The credibility today of the satirically funny drawings of Rowlandson and Hogarth may be due to the acceptable perspective of two centuries of time upon the harsh view of English life which they express. Contemporary satirists and cartoonists such as Gerald Scarfe and Ralph Steadman bathe in the warm glow of a public appreciation and enjoyment which does not extend to major one-man shows in the more prestigious galleries. One could even argue that early career success in a frivolous idiom for the artist and cartoonist Ronald Searle, may well have limited the direction his work has taken since; he has become an illustrator of some consequence, but the brilliance of his youthful portraits and other serious drawings has not been publicly celebrated quite as much as one might expect. Comic observations of contemporary life are enjoyed as trivialities but do not seem to be quite credible as art, indeed inhibit the recognition of their authors as artists. One can sympathize with the nineteenth-century artist, John Everett Millais, when as a young man he insisted that his drawings for the magazine *Punch* should appear unsigned, on the grounds that 'they would never go with the serious position I occupy in regard to art'.

To attempt to redeem and to encourage the humorous aspects of drawing in the art work of the young is, therefore, to move against the image of worthwhile art which is prevalent in our society. But I shall argue that humour is a natural and important constituent of creative experience for children, and especially accessible through drawing. Children keep on telling us this in their spontaneous drawing but we are not often alerted to the significance of their comic artefacts.

*   *   *

In *The Act of Creation*, Arthur Koestler presented a view of the creative process in three modes, all with the same 'logical pattern', the 'discovery of hidden similarities'. He argued that their differences lay in their 'emotional climates':

> the comic simile has a touch of aggressiveness; the scientist's reasoning by analogy is emotionally detached; the poetic image is sympathetic or admiring. (Koestler, 1971, p.27)

Within these different emotional modes, according to Koestler, the activities of science and the arts have 'fluid boundaries' or 'continuous gradients' as between, for instance, scientific truth and aesthetic experience, objective and subjective perception, utility and beauty. The boundaries between discovery and comic invention are, he reasons, particularly fluid with 'the Jester's riddles [providing] a useful backdoor entry as it were into the inner workshop of creative originality' (ibid., p.28).

So far as I am aware, Koestler did not discuss the degree to which this model of the creative process, with its continua of modes, is differently represented in the thinking of individuals. Such a model may be a description of an ideal, or of a psychological norm which exists in a deviated form in the minds and intellects of many. There is no doubt that in contemporary Western society, there is pressure arising from educational traditions in curriculum design to think in distinctively separate modes; while the connections exist in theory between scientific and aesthetic matters, many people are conditioned to perceive these as unconnected. Since conditioning is gradual, it is not unreasonable to suggest (and perhaps Koestler would have agreed) that the fluidity of the process he describes may be more familiar and natural to children than to adults, the latter tending to think less fluidly with increasing age unless study and experience determine otherwise. In the semi-autobiographical novel, *Zen and the Art of Motorcycle Maintenance*, Robert Pirzig (1974) vividly portrays both the awkwardness of an existence in which scientific and intuitive thinking do not come together and the way in which this is more of a problem for him than it is for his son.

An increasing separation of modes of creative thinking is in itself likely to impede the very quality of that thinking. As Koestler says, the ability to make connections of a new kind between previously disparate ideas, raises the level of mental activity; it achieves 'the defeat of habit by originality' (Koestler, 1971, p.98). But one may also argue that of the three creative domains which Koestler postulates, humour, discovery and art, the first of these is actively discouraged rather than fostered in childhood education. At an early stage in their lives, many children are quickly conditioned to the notion that humour, the only creative mode which generates physiological reflexive activity as well as potentially highly creative bisociative thinking, is inappropriate and irrelevant to learning.

*   *   *

From the generally low social valuing of humour, several beliefs are generated which affect school attitudes. Firstly, humour is commonly associated with leisure more than with work and learning. Secondly, the humourous content of children's comic drawings may be unwelcome because its aggressive and sometimes actually anarchic nature seems at odds with the seriousness of a prescribed curriculum. Thirdly, the stereotypic vernacular of imagery borrowed from a variety of sources and used in comic expression, seems to deny the traditions and conventions of academic drawing which are customarily preferred in the acquisition of drawing skills.

There is perhaps one further reason. Most primary school teachers in this country have been conditioned by received educational theory to expect a certain pattern of development in children's drawing. The earliest writers on drawing development in the present century (Sully, 1895; Luquet, 1913.) wrote of the young child in terms of inadequacy as an individual not yet metamorphosed into a satisfactory (adult) being, and of the child's apparent inability to draw realistically as a form of failure. Piagetian theory presented drawing as a mirror of the development of intellectual capacity, with the earliest drawing as largely originated by physical stimuli, gradually transmuting to reflect increasing 'active knowledge' of the real and tangible world (Piaget and Inhelder, 1969). Lowenfeld (1947), by far the most influential of writers on drawing and art education in Britain and the United States over the last thirty years, expressed greater awareness of the contribution of personal experience to expressive drawing than did Piaget, but nevertheless focused strongly on the attainment of realism, with imagination as a kind of inevitable casualty of expression in adolescence, if not before.

Until recently these ideas have been little questioned, but they have determined both the broad expectations of teachers and perhaps even indirectly the responses of many obliging children. The generalist teacher, uncertain of how drawing should be appraised, tends to regard early drawing as vigorous, often amusing or whimsical, but not actually important, and looks for signs of the development of realism, often valuing it more than expression and imaginative scenarios. The received 'wisdom' of the theories is long overdue for reappraisal in the light of what children really want to do and what they actually can do in drawing.

Children themselves, when unfettered by the demands of others, constantly reveal in their drawings the importance to them of humorous expression. Many do so from their earliest attempts to form images. In

Figure 7.1 (above): Drawing at four years, Charlotte

Figure 7.2 (below): Drawing at five years, Charlotte

Sylvia Fein's remarkable (1976) study of 'Heidi', the child's first representational sketches are of smiling faces and the first horse she manages to create in a drawing at four years has a distinct grin. The upturned curve of a mouth often combined with a round staring brightness of eyes seem to be first indications in many very young children's drawings of an attitude of benevolent amusement to the world. The positive intention to amuse frequently follows soon after the first achievement of these facial expressions. Many children soon discover ways of describing comic human character differences, for example, well before they can make conventional human figure drawings. Many intuitively exploit visually the typical bisociative phenomenon of the joke, by learning to combine two disparate and therefore jointly amusing ideas in one drawing. Even before school age is attained, a repertoire of comic drawing techniques is not unusual (Paine, 1985).

The humorous aspect of a drawing is not of course something which exists in isolation from its other intentions. Sometimes a particular structural technique may be employed, not only because it is amusing but because the visual joke points up a conceptual discovery, whether visual or abstract. Thus children teach themselves about form, space and movement, or social roles, perhaps by a drawn exaggeration of differences felt rather than observed. Sometimes a comic idea barely masks the underlying and maybe more important aggressive one, with the act of drawing having (possibly) some cathartic function for the child, and the humour making the image bearable. Actual fear seems sometimes to be ovecome in this manner, too (Paine, 1981). In the drawings of some young children, there exists a vein of comic-horror activity alongside a contrasting one of peaceful and contemplative observation. Nowhere is this more obvious than in the childhood drawings of the painter and printmaker, Michael Rothenstein, who remembers the conflicting delights of both modes of drawing. He describes hours spent on drawing the most decorative features of the plumage of birds or on 'the magic and mysterious world' of ponds and aquatic forms, but also describes his obsession with the 'joyful cruelty' of violence (Rothenstein, 1986).

Because humour is not always welcome at school, it may be perpetuated in drawings solely done at home and thus begin to exist as an almost separate but still important activity. But it does not always survive discouragement; some children who began to draw comically in early childhood, are deflected from continuing to do so by the desire to learn artistic conventions like everyone else at school. There is at least

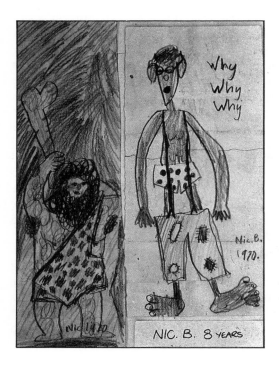

**Figure 7.3 and 7.4:
Drawings at eight
years, Nicholas**

Figure 7.5 (above): Drawing at six years, the contemporary artist, Michael Rothenstein (reproduced by courtesy of the Redstone Press)

Figure 7.6 (below): Drawing at 10/11 years, 'M'

one case, however, of a child who moved in the opposite direction, not having tried to draw amusingly in childhood but developing caricature and cartoon techniques quite deliberately at around nine years, because of anxiety about his skill to draw realistically. What was natural for some was in fact a conscious choice for him, and in this case it led to a deep involvement with caricature in adolescence and beyond. It should be said that his humorous drawings were mainly executed at home, where their reception was warmer (Paine, 1985).

*   *   *

The importance of comic expression as stimulus and device for creative originality seems evident in the work of many children and adolescents, however different their background and futures. But the pattern of its development and function varies. Humorous drawing can be seen as a lifelong interest in, for example, the work of the caricaturist Gerald Hoffnung. But for another and more eminent artist, Henri de Toulouse-Lautrec (1864-1901), comic sketches in childhood seemed to function as the base-activity for the development of a mature style. In adult life, his erotic, witty drawings were a private background subordinated to his artistic career and his major works often depended upon an element of caricature. The child 'Heidi' (Fein, 1976), on the other hand, had employed her early humorous work, it would appear, to seek her own identity in a world of people and animals; in adolescence, preoccupied with romanticizing and aesthetisizing her images, she seemed to have had no further need for the comical. A similar pattern is evident in another case: for 'M' (Paine, 1981) humour was clearly of interest and importance until, after about eleven years, he became consciously engrossed in learning to draw from nature, from the live model and from artefacts. The impact of all this attention to visual reality seemed to make human caricature rather less interesting to him than before. He directed himself more towards strong environmental and social statements, not dependent upon the distortion of appearances for their expression. But the intensive innovative and comic ideas of his childhood can be considered to have provided the foundation for his later expressive skill and fluency with the drawing media.

There are signs of a change in attitudes to children's humorous drawings at the present time, with, for example, the inclusion of much more that is witty and funny in national exhibitions of children's art. In some schools, too, classroom exhibits include amused or satirical responses to various experiences. But perhaps much of this material

**Figure 7.7:
Drawing at six
years, Henri de
Toulouse-Lautrec
(1864-1901)**

happens by chance and receives no positive encouragement from teachers or through the planned activities of the curriculum. Humour and its forms of expression rarely figure as the basis of topics for study in the primary school.

Yet there is a wealth of educative experience to be obtained from, for example, the comparison of methods of portrayals of the human figure by different professional cartoonists. Children with such experience can go on to analyse (by drawing) what makes one individual look different from another, and then to consider what such visual differences might convey about posture, role or character. Similar investigations can be conducted with the appearances of natural forms and with artefacts, to establish ways of indicating, by changes in the form of objects or by personification for example, their relationship with humans, whether spatial or symbolic.

Many quite young children show an interest in movement, one way according to Rousseau that we come to learn the difference between self and 'not-self' as well as gaining the idea of space (*Emile*, 1762). But in the first years at school, children's drawings typically become rather

Figure 7.8:
Drawing at
fourteen years,
Nicholas

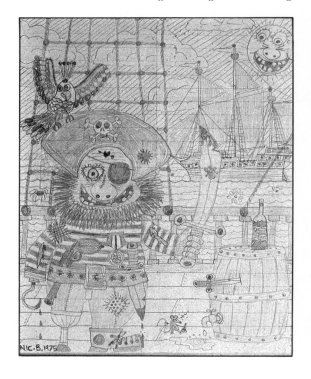

static. Cartoonists express movement, even in actually inanimate objects, by changing their shapes as well as by drawing movement traces in space. The investigation of such methods can have a very liberating effect upon the child's general capacity to adapt images for different expressive intentions. An important consequence, therefore, of this activity is the potential for the development of a rich and fluent personal visual language alongside an increasingly strong verbal one.

Children are of course individuals, differing in their needs and ideas. But it appears from their earliest spontaneous drawing that they nearly all at some time have a need to investigate their place in the world through the bisociative and potentially creative thinking involved in humorous expression. If obliged during their first years at school to conform to one particular style or method, they quickly become inhibited in drawing because they feel unable to use freely those forms of drawing which most naturally express their own ideas. Their need is to explore the full potential of the drawn image, especially its imaginative potential. Comic drawing effectively breaks the boundaries of convention in drawing and positively demands from its makers many acts of reconstruction, invention and appraisal which are fundamental educational experiences.

References

Bell, C. (1934), *Enjoying Pictures*. London: Chatto & Windus.

Fein, S. (1976), *Heidi's Horse*. California: Exelrod Press.

Inhelder, B. and Piaget, J. (1969), *The Psychology of the Child*. London: Routledge.

Koestler, A. (1971), *The Act of Creation*. London: Pan Books.

Löwenfeld, V. (1947), *Creative and Mental Growth*. New York: Macmillan.

Luquet, G. (1913), *Les Dessins d'un Enfant*. Paris: Librairie Felix Alcan.

Paine, S. (ed.) (1981), *Six Children Draw*. London: Academic Press.

Paine, S. (1985), 'The development of drawing in the childhood and adolescence of individuals', unpublished Ph.D. thesis. Institute of Education, University of London.

Pirzig, R. (1982), *Zen and the Art of Motorcycle Maintenance*. London: Bodley Head.

Rousseau, J.J. (1982), *Emile* (1762). London: J.M. Dent.

Rothenstein, J. (ed.) (1986), *Michael Rothenstein, Drawings and Paintings, Aged 4-9, 1912-1917*. London: Redstone Press.

Sully, J. (1903), *Studies of Childhood* (1895). London: Longmans, Green & Co.

Chapter Eight
Learning About Art
Anthony Dyson

It will hardly be necessary to persuade readers of this book about the value, of giving young children opportunities to learn *about* art as well as to engage *in* it. The Gulbenkian Report, *The Arts in Schools*, (1982) gave eloquent emphasis to the importance in all the arts of a partnership of participation and appreciation; and, more recently, the work of A.R. Taylor, culminating in the account (Taylor, 1986) of a national project on critical studies in schools, has provided for the field of visual art rich substantiation for the proposal that looking and responding to objects and images is no less vital a part of a child's art education than is the doing and making whose contribution have long been acknowledged in our schools.

I have argued elsewhere (Dyson, 1982) for a comprehensive strategy where the acquisition of knowledge and the development of critical skills are concerned, and have done so in the belief that we should devise some systematic means (just as, ideally, in practical art activity) of leading pupils, through their years of general education, towards some understanding of that complex, infinitely varied phenomenon, Art. Invoking Jerome Bruner's spiral curriculum, his notion of revisiting (and thus deepening) areas of knowledge and understanding at successive stages in a pupil's schooling (fully elaborated in *The Process of Education*, 1962), I suggested that it is never too soon to begin involving children in contemplating and discussing art objects. The mundane visual experience can provide a springboard: comparisons of everyday sights with art objects having some formal, metaphorical, narrative, or other connection, would, I argued, provide a sensible introduction to increasingly rigorous visual challenges, culminating in some understanding of the interconnectedness of the aesthetic, technical, social, biographical, and other ramifications of art objects — of whatever period or culture. I argued this procedure as a means of providing a sound apprenticeship for those wishing eventually to progress to a more advanced study of the subject in further or higher education; but also as an illuminating educational experience in itself for those with no particular vocational aspirations in the field of art.

How could a course for primary school pupils and those in the early years of secondary school be structured, and how might it provide an appropriate modulation from the encouragement of general visual sensitivity to a more specialized knowledge of art? It would seem valuable to base the approach on a series of comparisons. The technique of comparison is widely used in art history teaching in higher education. Inviting students to seek similarities and differences in related images is an effective means of compelling them to look and think. In presenting comparisons to children, at least two factors need to be kept in mind: first, that we can learn much from pupils' responses to what we show them, and would be well advised to heed these promptings in any selection we may make; and second, that sharply contrasting images are perhaps likelier than closely similar ones to provide an effective starting point for younger pupils. The first consideration scarcely needs amplifying: a flexible attitude on the part of the teacher and the avoidance of stock comparisons (with the attendant risk of deadening experience and blunting perception), and involving pupils in discussion so that they may more readily develop a framework of language to assist understanding, are clearly desirable. Any student of linguistics will confirm the importance of the second: to attempt to teach a person the meaning of the word 'brown' by presenting to him only brown objects (however many and in however many shades of the colour) will prove infinitely more frustrating for both teacher and pupil than contrasting the brown with objects of other hue. The brownness — and, incidentally, the blueness, yellowness, or redness of the objects juxtaposed with the brown — will thus become more easily graspable and the link between the word and the perceptual experience it signifies will be more surely forged. Brown is brown by virtue of all the other colours it is not; a Cubist painting is a Cubist painting by virtue of the fact that it is not an Impressionist or a Fauve or a Futurist or any other kind of painting. Furthermore, a Cubist painting by Picasso is recognizable as such by virtue of the fact that it is not a painting by Braque or any other Cubist — but this, of course, is where things get difficult!

The structure of the history of art is not immutable. It is a matter for proposal by individual scholars. Similarly, the shaping of the practically limitless volume of visual material that could feasibly be used in schools is a matter for initiation by individual teachers. A heavy reliance on 'packaged' material and a dependence on what have been referred to as 'teacher-proof curricula' are the very antithesis of the flexible approach most likely to stimulate the interest of pupils. Doing a little sorting exercise with a hundred (or more) postcard reproductions of paintings can be a valuable step in the direction of the structuring process. What might the possible criteria for classification be? What about the polarity complexity/simplicity? Having decided which is the most complex image and which the simplest (and if the exercise is undertaken by two or more persons there is sure to be considerable debate on the matter of selection) the business of arranging all the other images on a scale from complexity to simplicity could be tackled. Other polarities such as crudeness/refinement; verticality/horizontality, order/chaos, obscurity/ definition, lightness/darkness, depth/flatness are further possibilities.

★   ★   ★

The foregoing is proposed simply by way of encouragement to teachers to proceed with confidence; and to emphasize that what is offered below is suggestion rather than prescription.

Consider the following categories of comparison:

1. *A comparison of reproductions of art objects with visual records of experience familiar to pupils, or with everyday objects.*
An example of this kind of comparison might be a photograph of a greengrocer's stall set alongside one of a Byzantine mosaic. This might give rise to such questions as:

In what ways are the images alike?
In what ways are they different?
Why should one be thought a work of art, the other not?

2. *A comparison of different art objects each with similar subject matter (or different buildings erected for a similar purpose).*
Examples of this kind of comparison might be a printed reproduction (or a transparency, of course) of a Cubist head and a Renaissance portrait juxtaposed; or the Roman Colosseum set beside Wembley Stadium. In addition to the fundamental questions regarding difference and similarity, others are likely to be raised, including:

How were the respective items made?
By what kind of person or persons was each made?
For what kind of person or persons was each made?
For what purpose might each have been made?

3. *A comparison of pupils' own work in art with appropriate art objects.*
The whole matter of the integration of the production and the appraisal of art in schools deserves full and separate treatment. The opportunities offered by such links may be hinted at by the following questions:

How do I draw (or otherwise represent or express) the things I see (or imagine)?
How do I feel about the things I see (or imagine)?
Do my drawings look 'real'?
Do I intend them to look real?
How can I make them look more real?
Are there artists whose work mine resembles?
In what ways?
Are there ways of drawing other than mine?
How do different artists draw?
What makes them draw differently?
Do different artists see differently?
Do they think differently?
Is it this that makes them draw differently?

4. *A comparison of artefacts of different periods.*
Questions such as these might spring from this kind of comparison:

When might each item have been made?
Recently?
Long ago?
About how long ago?
What evidence that it is old or recently made does each contain?
How might a number of items be arranged chronologically?
What could such an arrangement tell us about changes in how people see or in what they like?

5. *A comparison of various products of a particular period: choice not restricted to art objects, nor even to visual material.*
Study based on comparisons of this kind could lead to a realization of the essential 'untidiness' of history. If, for example, a coronation

photograph of Edward VII and Alexandra were to be shown beside a
Fauve painting produced at more or less the same moment in history; or
if a poster advertising an early motor car were to be juxtaposed with a
photograph of, say, Boccioni's sculpture 'Unique forms of continuity in
space' (1913), something of the *avant-garde* nature of the chosen art
objects might more clearly be seen by pupils, and the bewilderment
experienced by contemporaries could be sensed more deeply. A
consideration of such material could give rise to questions such as:

When does each item look as if it was produced?
What evidence of date is to be found in the item itself; and what
related evidence is available?
Do any items appear to be 'ahead of their time'?
Or 'behind the times'?
Is there such a thing as 'the spirit of an age'?
Would any particular object — or depiction — have been possible at
any period other than the one in which it was produced?
Or in any other place?

6.   *A comparison of art objects of a given School or period.*
This is the kind of task facing most prospective examination candidates,
who will need to consider such questions as:

In what ways are the works similar?
In what ways are they different?
Are there stronger 'family resemblances' between the works of this
period (or School, or culture) than between those of other periods?
Or is the opposite the case?
Has the artist any importance as an individual during the period
under review?
Assuming he can be identified as an individual, how does what we
know about him influence the way we view his work?
How does the work of one artist seem to have influenced that of
another?

*   *   *

I have also suggested, in another context (Dyson, 1984), that the much-
maligned activity of copying can contribute effectively to a child's
knowledge and understanding of art. Since copying has been for many
of the most celebrated artists in history a salutary means of study why, I

wonder, should it not have its perfectly respectable uses in schools? In his book *Ideals and Idols* (1979), E.H. Gombrich reproduces an interesting exchange of correspondence with Quentin Bell, who was then Professor of Fine Art at the University of Sussex. In one letter, Gombrich remarked that a teacher he knew had argued that art is 'creativity' and that, this being so, it could not be taught. Bell replied that he had once worked in a primary school, where he had shocked another member of staff by inviting his pupils to make copies of reproductions of Raphael's paintings. Stimulated by these reproductions, the children had made extremely beautiful drawings. Predictably, they had not imitated — probably not even perceived — Raphael's characteristically subtle rendering of volume: their interpretations had more of the flatness of a Simone Martini. The scandalized colleague reacted as though the children's artistic virginity had been violated by this requirement to copy from reproductions. Bell's retort was that his pupils' supposed visual innocence had already been lost many times over since infancy, through constant exposure to influences beneficial and otherwise. The Raphael exercise at least concentrated their attention on exemplars of high quality. It was an exercise demanding hand and eye co-ordination, and it was for the pupils an early experience of the study of art — an experience that could with similar teaching profitably be built upon during their subsequent years of schooling. Alas, for most pupils it is an experience that is all too seldom encouraged.

Part of the problem is that children's art has for the last few decades been a subject of study by psychologists rather than by artists, and by art educators whose interests are psychological rather than aesthetic. Psychologists (Rudolf Arnheim, for example) have produced much influential writing which, whilst it is of course excellent in its own way, has in a sense been inhibiting for teachers of young children. During their training, most intending primary school teachers will have studied a considerable volume of psychological material referring to children's art but, unless specialists in the subject, will scarcely have studied art itself. It is little wonder, then, that many teachers feel their duty is fulfilled if they simply provide picture-making materials and perhaps a title or two (and what a relief it is when Guy Fawkes or Christmas festivities automatically provide subjects!), urge their pupils to 'use their imaginations', and stand back — even if only metaphorically — and await the pictorial outcome. This, at least if the children are young enough, will infallibly by charming; and this charm seems to confirm still more strongly the conviction that young children's art activity is 'not to be interfered with'.

It is not appropriate at this point to become two embroiled in those difficult and elusive concepts indicated by the words 'originality', 'imagination' and 'creativity'; writers such as R.F. Dearden (1968) have dealt admirably and concisely with such issues. It will be enough for the moment to suggest that there still persists an idea that, if given opportunities and facilities and, above all, a freedom from 'inhibiting instruction', pupils will be more likely to give form to 'original ideas', will be allowed greater scope for the exercise of the imagination, and will give fuller expression to an 'innate' creativity. Those holding such views will accordingly shrink from the idea of copying, ignoring its usefulness as a means of helping pupils to study and come more fully to understand the work of others more accomplished than themselves. There is of course room in a child's experience for art as expression; it will be salutary, too, to make room for art as investigation. Artists have, by and large, always been avid students of the work of their colleagues, as a glance at the letters of Van Gogh or the journal of Delacroix will show. Even artists like Wassily Kandinsky or Paul Klee, who might often be seen as the very embodiments of the cult of artistic self-sufficiency, clearly developed their craft on the basis of such study. (The word 'craft' is not, incidentally, used casually here. One of the arguments of this chapter is precisely that the element of craftsmanship, of sheer know-how, is in urgent need of reinstatement in art education — in spite of the fact that it was admittedly given unduly feverish attention in even the best of nineteenth-century art education.)

Let us look squarely at the business of copying. It is often thought to be damaging — but why? Is it possible that this has become one of those mysterious taboos — like drawing with a ruler, or using a rubber — that is strictly observed for no analysable reason? The argument seems to be that copying militates against a pupil's own inventiveness, or, at least, that time spent copying would be far better spent 'expressing' personal ideas. The attitude is perhaps descended from that of the founders of the Royal Academy, who for a hundred years refused to grant full membership to those professional copyists, the reproductive engravers, on the grounds that invention was the prerogative of the true artist, whilst engravers were merely a 'set of ingenious mechanics'. R.F. Dearden (1968) has pointed out that unless children are given opportunities to come to know, for example, the poetry of others generally acknowledged to be competent in their craft, they are hardly likely to develop any concept of what a poem is. I suggest that one of the most effective ways of coming to know works of visual art is to engage in

Figure 8.1: Seven-year old's copy of a portrait reproduction

that most salutary form of note-taking: copying (and the word is here given its full range of meanings — replicating, emulating, reproducing, interpreting). Although the European Romantic tradition (other cultures seem not to share this particular difficulty), in so far as it has embodied the cult of the individual, has tended to obscure the fact, most artisits have always learned from each other in this way. There exist, for example, 'copies' of Persian miniatures by Rembrandt, 'copies' of Rembrandt by Van Gogh, 'copies' of Van Gogh by Francis Bacon ... If this were not the case, there could hardly be such a thing as 'the history of art'. If there were no such influences, and corresponding emulations, all would be the work of idiosyncratic individuals constantly re-inventing art, and the broad patterns on which the writer of history depends (or seeks to discern) would be absent.

★   ★   ★

There seems to me to be a vital distinction between the kind of drawing that comes about as naturally as speech, and that which is (but not at all in a derogatory sense) contrived; between that form of drawing which is the descendant of instinctive infant scribble, engaged in by all children regardless of whether or not orthodox art materials are available, and that form of drawing which embodies consciously-adopted conventions; between that which comes about whether tutored or not, and that which is nurtured by the deliberate acquisition of taught skills. Adherents of what has come to be known as 'child-centred' education seem to have been mesmerized by the former, and to frown on the latter as being against the natural inclination of chidren. Art, it is frequently forgotten, is a matter of the employment of convention; and, as such, there is very little about it that is 'natural'. Art is, in a very important sense, artifical. John Constable (who, ironically, is popularly renowned for his naturalness) knew this better than most: 'the Art pleases by reminding, not by deceiving', he pointed out. No artist mastered more fully that sleight of hand which transforms flicks of paint into a reminiscence of things seen in nature; no artist was more completely aware of the need for conscientious study as a means of attaining that mastery; no artist showed us more clearly the fallacy of the idea that visual experience can, simply given sufficient skill, be represented in pictorial facsimile.

These two forms of drawing — 'natural' and 'contrived' — are, though distinguishable, related. In fact, the 'natural' and the 'contrived' co-exist in the drawings of most mature artists. In so far as the 'natural' is less consciously controlled, it is to a large extent this element in a drawing (or painting, or sculpture) that determines what we call style — the artist's 'handwriting'.

Children who are ultimately identified as having facility in drawing begin to make a transition from the 'natural', less conscious form of drawing, to the 'contrived', more consciously controlled form, quite early — often around the age of seven or eight. The shift of emphasis is frequently assisted by copying. And the images that are copied are, naturally, those that come most readily to hand: comic caricatures, advertising graphics, and so on. Our reluctance to involve children in copying (Quentin Bell's sin against the innocence of child draughtsmanship!) comes about through an exaggerated respect for 'natural' drawing. Inevitably, sooner or later, children will seek to emulate the drawings of others; and we should welcome this rather than discourage it. It provides a golden opportunity to engage pupils in the serious study of art. 'Natural' drawing has its place in the infant school and well beyond; but I should here like to propose that our scruples about interfering with the innocence of 'natural' childish drawing is at the root of our failure to include in the art education of almost all pupils up to the age of sixteen an adequate element of appraisal. It is at the root of the traditional separation in education of what, as we have seen, the Gulbenkian Report refers to as 'experience' and 'appreciation', the separation of practical art from the history, criticism and appreciation of art.

*   *   *

The writer's recent experimental work with two classes of primary school children (ages 7 - 8 and 9 - 10) was based on the premise that the fusion of experience and appreciation should begin at least by the time a child is seven. It was based on the principle of studying art. In setting up the experiment, it seemed important that the work be undertaken in circumstances as realistic as possible. Accordingly, a school catering for children from a variety of social and cultural backgrounds was chosen; full classes of about thirty children were taught; the normal school timetable was adhered to; and no special materials or equipment (not even a slide projector) were used.

The chief source of visual stimulus was a large collection of postcard reproductions of drawings, engravings, paintings, sculpture, architecture, furniture, musical instruments and other artefacts. This was supplemented by a few examples of 'the real thing': an oil painting, an engraved wood-block, and an etched metal plate with corresponding print, for example. Besides relative inexpensiveness, the collection of postcard reproductions had certain very important advantages over books and slides, and complemented the appraisal of original art objects in valuable ways. The most prominent advantage was that the reproductions could be grouped and classified and compared in endless ways. This flexibility provided an ideal basis for discussion with individuals, between the members of small groups of pupils, and with the class as a whole. The paintings, plates, blocks and prints made it possible to begin to develop pupils' insights into the relationship between the real thing and reproductions of it; made it possible to discuss the distinction between photographic reproduction and, say, engraved reproduction; and, with appropriate reproductions, they provided an effective introduction to the gallery visit which was to be a culmination of the experiment.

Many pupils in both classes were capable of a high level of discussion of the relationship between things seen in nature, original representations of these visual experiences, and reproductions of the originals. When the 7-8 year-olds were shown a small oil painting of a boat on a beach and were asked simply, 'What is this?', the reply, 'It's a boat', was very promptly contradicted by the protest 'No, it's a *picture* of a boat.' It was then but a small step to the notion of a 'photograph of a picture of a boat', fortified by a comparison of the texture of an original and the texturelessness of a photographic reproduction. When the children were given a magnifying glass and asked, 'How was this picture made?', there was no doubt that their careful scrutiny (and fingering) of the object reinforced their notion of an artefact — an artefact not dissimilar to their own paintings; no doubt that it was at least a first step towards their sense of community with artists and craftsmen. The discussion of originals and reproductions led to the matter of relative scale. One 7 year-old discovered two reproductions of the same painting by George Stubbs. The reproductions were different in size, one being printed on a leaf of a large calendar, the other being a postcard version. On the back of the postcard were printed the dimensions of the original painting in the National Gallery. With this information, a rectangle the exact size of the original was drawn on the blackboard, and the two reproductions were placed like postage stamps in its corners.

Throughout the discussions with children, careful attention was given to the matter of accurate terminology. For example, a clear distinction was made between the word 'copying' (in the sense of making a single re-presentation) and the word 'reproducing' (in the sense of making something capable of identical repetition). There are, of course, subtle overlaps of meaning that young children can hardly be expected to grasp; but if, with Jerome Bruner, we believe that the essence of an idea introduced to young children can be 'revisited' with increasing degrees of sophistication throughout their subsequent schooling, there seems no good reason for delay. Pupils were helped to make such distinctions as this by making 'one-off' copies in a variety of media, and by making their own printed reproductions (in the tradition of the eighteenth- and nineteenth-century engravers) of postcard images from linoleum blocks.

As the work progressed, it became increasingly evident that there was a pronounced interdependence of experiences: an interdependence of one practical enterprise with another; of practical experience with discussion, appraisal and response; of one concept with another. This was particularly clear in one project involving the 7 - 8 year-olds. Each child was given three portrait reproductions: one 'modern' (incorporating the usual liberties with colour, handling, etc.); one 'traditional' (highly illusionistic); and one schematic (with very clear,

Figure 8.2 (above): Nine-year olds' linocut reproductions of portraits

Figure 8.3 (below): A nine-year old comparing with the original painting a postcard reproduction he has been studying in school

emphasized line). In the first place, the children were asked to arrange the reproductions chronologically: the oldest on the left, the newest on the right. What ensued was a salutary reminder of the importance of the teacher's awareness of his own need for vigilance in the use of language. For example, Samantha considered a twentieth-century painting by Walter Sickert to be 'older' than a portrait of Elizabeth I. It transpired during discussion that the child had interpreted the words 'old' and 'new' not in the chronological sense intended by the teacher, but in the sense of 'used' and 'pristine'! And there was certainly a drabness about the Sickert and a brilliance of colour in the Tudor painting that made the little girl's decision eminently logical.

One aim of the project was, however, to see if these young children could detect any evidence for chronological placing. Accuracy of dating was, of course, neither expected not sought; chronological sequence was considered enough. This was a particularly fascinating exercise, because it revealed so much that (to invoke Bruner again) was a potential foundation for subsequent learning. The children were all quite confident that the portrait of Anne Boleyn was painted 'long ago'; their estimates of just how long ranged from 10 to 1,000 years. One boy suggested the almost correct figure of 500 years, and when asked why, he answered after some pondering that he had based his estimate on his seven years' experience of the world, and had multiplied this to what he considered a feasible extent. One might well be tempted to smile condescendingly at all this, but it was a valuable beginning. Another example: Benjamin did not doubt that the portrait of Shakespeare was earlier than that of Churchill. Shakespeare, he noticed, wore 'old-fashioned' clothes; and his comment that the Churchill portrait 'looks like it's just been painted' seemed to denote an acute perception of the artist's vigorous brushwork. There were other salutary reminders to the teacher of the need for care in selecting resources: one pupil decided that a portrait of Gaudier-Brzeska (20th c.), reproduced in monochrome, was older than the sixteenth-century portrait of Henry Howard because 'in the olden days they used to use black and white'!

Another preconception dismantled by the children was this: I have argued above for a comparative approach to the study of art objects, and have suggested that it makes good sense to present younger children with sharply contrasting images whose differences they can readily spot — pictures by Picasso and by Leonardo da Vinci, for example. However, Christopher (aged 9) selected from a number of reproductions of flower paintings, in a wide range of styles, two very similar Dutch seventeenth-century pictures, and spent a whole hour

Figure 8.4: A seven-year old studies three portrait reproductions

carefully comparing them and listing the differences and similarities.

It is vital that children have frequent opportunities of working from direct experience, of making drawings and paintings from objects they can handle, and of environments in which they can move. These are extremely important ways of coming to appreciate such properties as texture, structure, space, and volume. But my proposal is simply this: that studying art objects and images is an effective vehicle of learning for young children; that such study can be more sharply focused through that activity deprecatingly called copying; and that working in this way may assist inventiveness. It certainly will not inhibit it.

*   *   *

More recent reflection on the subject of pupils' copying has led me to the conclusion that the potential benefits are at least two-fold: as well as children being helped thereby to understand artistic convention, their copies of images and artefacts can teach *us*, giving us insights not only into how the children perceive those visual puzzles we call pictures, but also into the nature of pictorial art itself. E.H. Gombrich has pointed to the 'universal tendency among image-makers of all periods and cultures to transpose a 3D view into a 2D code' and to 'the transformations realistic paintings and prints undergo when copied by artists not trained in 3D skills' and also to the fact that many styles in the history of art share certain structural characteristics 'with the art of the unskilled and of children' (Gombrich, 1985). Here, I shall refer almost exclusively to the children's pictorial work, for it is in their copies of pictures and photographs that we may observe those transformations that could help us to look afresh at certain conventions that we now, in the West at least, seem to take for granted.

I return to the exercise with the three postcard reproductions (referred to on p.120, above). In this exercise, each child was faced with three different artists' transpositions of a three-dimensional view (in this case, of a human sitter) into a two-dimensional 'code'; and what became deeply interesting for me was what the children seemed to reveal of *their* grasp of the pictorial conventions entailed — or of their failure (often quite understandably) to do so. As part of the exercise in question, the children were invited to choose any one of the three cards to copy. I simply wondered if they would tend towards the sharply linear portraits rather than towards the tonally gradated, towards the more diagrammatically simple than towards the more illusionistic. It is upon these choices and upon the resulting highly significant copies that I should now like to concentrate.

First, the matter of choice. Here I propose a distinction between *preference* ('liking' for a particular image) and *selection* of a particular image for copying. That there is such a distinction remains to be tested. I discovered that the children by no means always chose to copy the most schematic image, but what they always did (perhaps predictably) was *render* the chosen image schematically. When, on other occasions, each child was given a larger number of stylistically contrasting portraits and was invited to copy all of them, little, if any, awareness of these stylistic differences was evident in the drawings: all, whether schematic or naturalistic, were rendered schematically. Each child's group of drawings had a strong 'family' resemblance, and this family likeness was much more pronounced than any resemblance to the images being copied. This suggests the hypothesis that stylistic differences in pictorial imagery are not easily perceived by children of this age, but that through language (and possibly through other experiences) the development of such perception may be accelerated.

And now, the copies. Perhaps two examples will be sufficient: a copy of a self-portrait by Vincent Van Gogh; and one of a self-portrait by Thomas Gainsborough. Both portraits adopt the commonplace Western convention of the three-quarter view, depicting head and shoulders against a background. In neither case could the seven year-old copyist handle the three-quarter angle of the head; each interpreted this as a full-face view. And in neither case, evidently, did the young transposer fully grasp the convention of the truncation of the body by the bottom edge of the picture.

In the Van Gogh portrait, the artist's coat gapes open below the single button fastened at the throat. This painting of the coat forms, with the bottom edge of the canvas, a triangle. It seems clear that Van Gogh's use of this 'guillotining' convention has not been understood by the child, who has transformed the triangular shape into a kind of medallion hanging beneath the coat button.

Scott's transfiguration of the Gainsborough is even more drastic: the truncated head and shoulders portrait is, in his version, detached from the bottom edge of the picture, and the background of foliage has become a scattering of plant images, forming a kind of elaborated frame around the sitter.

In neither case is it suggested that the child's copy is in any way inadequate: each has its logic. It is simply that neither artists' pictorial logic has been accurately 'read' by the child. Pictorial logic is something that can only be learned by studying pictures, rather as one has to study a foreign language. There is nothing 'natural' about it; one simply has to learn the 'code'. And learning *about* art — about the essential artificiality of art — is in my view an important ingredient in any child's art education.

*   *   *

Among the writers whose work I have found illuminating in this connection are: E.H. Gombrich, already referred to several times; John Baines, of the Oriental Institute, University of Oxford; John M. Kennedy, of Victoria University, Toronto; and Alan Gowans, of the University of Victoria, British Columbia.

Gombrich points out that

> all representation can be ... arranged along a scale ... from the schematic to the impressionist ... there exists a natural pull toward the schematic which artists such as Giotto or Constable succeeded in overcoming. Because of this gravitation toward the schematic or 'conceptual', we have a right to speak of

Figure 8.5 (above): A seven-year old's study of a Van Gogh self-portrait

Figure 8.6 (below): Scott (aged seven) and his interpretation of the Gainsborough self-portrait

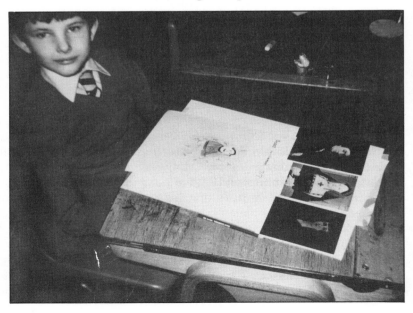

'primitive' modes of representation, modes, that is, which assert themselves unless they are deliberately counteracted. (Gombrich, quoted in Baines, 1985, p.17)

I suggested that what we see in the drawings of these 7-8 year-olds is simply evidence of this 'natural pull toward the schematic', a pull which will (but perhaps not in every case) be counteracted through various cultural influences, including teaching. John Baines himself goes on to say that

Gombrich's 'pull' is in part technical — the schematic is more easily executed than the variability of foreshortening — and this relates in turn to the status of representation as a system of signs at a greatly reduced scale from reality. Any particular system of non-perspective representation is one culture's [or one child's?] version of this universal. (ibid.)

Baines proceeds to propose an 'evolutionary' universal:

(i) Schematic; (ii) 'Realistic'; (iii) Incorporation of foreshortening and use of oblique projective systems; and (iv) Perspective. The four stages ... map the complete transition from object-centred to viewer-centred representation. (ibid.)

His challenging article concludes with the contention that

non-perspective is the natural and universal form of representation ... Whereas the comprehension of non-perspective representation offers a challenge only to modern westerners, the move away from it ... needs explanation, because it is so exceptional in the global history of art. (ibid.)

He also makes the interesting observation that 'as a system of representation, perspective is culturally neutral'.

Gombrich incidentally, was intrigued (in *Art and Illusion*) by the question of why naturalistic representation (of which a vital component is perspective, atmospheric and linear) should have a history at all, 'why what we find in certain periods of the history of art like that of ancient Greece or the Renaissance, resembles a learning process ...' and proposed that 'when the social function of images is expected to serve illusionism — whatever we may mean by this slippery term — that goal can only be reached by trial and error, by the slow and systematic modification of schematic images till they match the motif they are meant to represent' (Gombrich, 1984, p.15). Elsewhere, he has discussed the puzzle of the discrepancy between 'making' and 'matching' (Gombrich, 1985). Referring to the work of the anthropologist Franz Boas, who in his book on *Primitive Art* (1972) insisted that tribal artists are capable of attaining 'realistic truth' — an observation that seems to be lent plausibility by such lifelike sculptures as those from Ife — he pointed to the vital distinction between reproducing in the round a three-dimensional object, and 'reproducing' pictorially, in two dimensions, a spatial prospect. What has never been systematically explored, as far as I know, is the relationship between the imitative capacity in three- and two-dimensional work of individual children. A hypothesis might be formulated as follows: that young children (given appropriate technical support) can more faithfully reproduce in three dimensions than in two; that the 'schematic pull' referred to earlier is stronger in the two-dimensional than in the three-dimensional field; and that in the latter, tactile and kinetic experience play a decisive part.

The importance of tactile and kinetic experience is borne out by the work of John Kennedy. In his accounts (1984, 1985) of many years' research with congenitally blind children and adults he seeks to establish that pictures are more the result of universal 'givens' than of visually acquired conventions. We do not have to learn to read a caveman's drawing: its elements of line, perspective, metaphor, and expression are, he suggests, universally communicable. Recognition of these elements, and the capacity to read them pictorially, is awakened rather than imbued, he proposes, and he seeks to substantiate this through observations based on raised-line drawings by blind people — to discover through these drawings what the blind know of a world assumed by the sighted to be predominantly visual. Lines in pictures stand for the tangible; they denote changes of plane, interruptions of surface, edges of objects, and so on, so that when a blind person can feel, he or she can draw. (This seems to lead to a further hypothesis: that, if Kennedy's theory of universals is correct, tactile and kinetic experience may play a far more prominent part in juvenile drawing than is usually recognized). Pespective is defined by Kennedy as the science of the direction of objects, whether perceived visually by light travelling in to the eye, or by touch moving out; and he has many drawings (including one of a table 'viewed' from below) which seem to support his claim that blind people understand perspective. He also demonstrates their grasp of pictorial metaphor and expression with, for example, drawings by them of wheels in motion, the spokes curved to suggest speed. Perhaps what has been referred to by Lowenfeld and others as the haptic inclination of some children's drawings is as plausibly explained by the notion of pictorial metaphor?

The whole question of the relationship of children's art to adult art deserves fuller examination, whether or not such examination occurs within the framework of an 'ontogeny repeats phylogeny' thesis. Alan Gowans (1979) has proposed child art as an instrument for studying history: the development of an individual human consciousness parallels that of the whole human race, he maintains. He points out that the traditional social functions of art (making substitute images; illustrating; beautifying; and persuading and convincing) have been lost in *avant-garde* fine art, but that they are perpetuated in primitive, popular, commercial, and children's art. He goes on to attempt a correlation between children's mental growth (invoking Piaget's theories of conceptual development) and the evolution of art in history. Gowans' suggestion is that present-day *avant-garde* art defies definition: art is, simply, what artists say it is. If this is so (and the foundation of much *avant-garde* art certainly seems to me to be unlocatable, not to say unstable) one is led to question the use of such work as a basis for children's initiation into an understanding of the concept 'art'.

Examined closely, the views of the four authors I have referred to will be seen by no means to coincide tidily; their value has for me been essentially catalytic. In summary, they have left me — as I leave the reader — with these questions. What, if any, is the distinction between a child's preference for a particular image or category of images, and the 'natural pull' that results in schematic drawing? How may children's ability to perceive stylistic differences in pictorial art be gauged? How may a child's imitative capacity in three- and two-dimensional media be compared? What is the role of tactile and kinetic experience in a child's drawing development? What is the role of metaphor in a child's drawing development? And what is the value of *avante-garde* art (as against that with a clearly-perceivable social function) as a basis for a child's development of the concept, 'art'?

Note
By kind permission of the National Society for Education in Art and Design, this chapter is substantially based on material from three of my papers published in the Society's *Journal of Art and Design Education*. They are: 'Art history in schools: a comprehensive strategy', Vol.1, No.1, 1982; 'Originality and originals, copies and reproductions: reflections on a primary school project', Vol.3, No.2, 1984; and 'The three-card trick: the reading of images by young children', Vol.5, Nos 1 and 2, 1986.

References

Baines, J. (1985), 'Theories and universals of representation: Heinrich Schafer and Egyptian art', *Art History*, Vol.8, No.1.

Bruner, J. (1962), *The Process of Education*. Cambridge, Mass.: Harvard University Press.

Dearden, R.F. (1968), *The Philosophy of Primary Education*. London: Routledge.

Dyson, A. (1982) 'Art history in schools: a comprehensive strategy', *Journal of Art and Design Education*, Vol.1, No.1.

_____ (1984), 'Originality and originals, copies and reproductions: reflections on a primary school project', *Journal of Art and Design Education*, Vol.3, No.2.

Gombrich, E.H. (1979), *Ideals and Idols*. Oxford: Phaidon.

_____ (1984), Tributes. Oxford: Phaidon.

_____ (1985), 'Making and matching: 3D and 2D', conference paper. Association of Art Historians, London.

Gowans, A. (1979), 'Child art as an instrument for studying history', *Art History*, Vol.2, No.3,

Gulbenkian Report (1982), *The Arts in Schools*. London: Gulbenkian Foundation.

Kennedy, J.M. (1984), *Vision and Metaphor: empirical investigations.* Toronto: Victoria University.

_____ (1985), 'Art, vision and pictures by the blind', conference paper. Association of Art Historians, London.

Bedford Way Papers

ISSN 0261—0078

1. 'Fifteen Thousand Hours': A Discussion
Barbara Tizard *et al.*
ISBN 0 85473 090 7

3. Issues in Music Education
Charles Plummeridge *et al.*
ISBN 0 85473 105 9

4. No Minister: A Critique of the D E S
Paper 'The School Curriculum'
John White *et al.*
ISBN 0 85473 115 6

5. Publishing School Examination
Results: A Discussion
Ian Plewis *et al.*
ISBN 0 85473 116 4

8. Girls and Mathematics: The Early Years
Rosie Walden and Valerie Walkerdine
ISBN 0 85473 124 5

9. Reorganisation of Secondary
Education in Manchester
Dudley Fiske
ISBN 0 85473 125 3

11. The Language Monitors
Harold Rosen
ISBN 0 85473 134 2

13. Geography in Education Now
Norman Graves *et al.*
ISBN 0 85473 219 5

14. Art and Design Education:
Heritage and Prospect
Anthony Dyson *et al.*
ISBN 0 85473 245 4

15. Is Teaching a Profession?
Peter Gordon (ed.)
ISBN 0 85473 220 9

16. Teaching Political Literacy
Alex Porter (ed.)
ISBN 0 85473 154 7

17. Opening Moves: Study of Children's
Language Development
Margaret Meek (ed.)
ISBN 0 85473 161 X

18. Secondary School Examinations
Jo Mortimore, Peter Mortimore and
Clyde Chitty
ISBN 0 85473 259 4

19. Lessons Before Midnight:
Educating for Reason in Nuclear Matters
The Bishop of Salisbury *et al.*
ISBN 0 85473 189 X

20. Education plc?: Headteachers
and the New Training Initiative
Janet Maw *et al.*
ISBN 0 85473 191 1

21. The Tightening Grip: Growth of Central
Control of the School Curriculum
Denis Lawton
ISBN 0 85473 201 2

22. The Quality Controllers: A Critique of
the White Paper 'Teaching Quality'
Frances Slater (ed.)
ISBN 0 85473 212 8

23. Education: Time for a New Act?
Richard Aldrich and Patricia Leighton
ISBN 0 85473 217 9

24. Girls and Mathematics: from Primary to
Secondary Schooling
Rosie Walden and Valerie Walkerdine
ISBN 0 85473 222 5

25. Psychology and Schooling:
What's the Matter?
Guy Claxton *et al.*
ISBN 0 85473 228 4

26. Sarah's Letters: A Case of Shyness
Bernard T. Harrison
ISBN 0 85473 241 1

27. The Infant School:
past, present and future
Rosemary Davis (ed.)
ISBN 0 85473 250 0

28. The Politics of Health Information
Wendy Farrant and Jill Russell
ISBN 0 85473 260 8

29. The GCSE: and uncommon examination
Caroline Gipps (ed.)
ISBN 0 85473 262 4

30. Education for a Pluralist Society
Graham Haydon (ed.)
ISBN 0 85473 263 2

31. Lessons in Partnership:
and INSET course as a case study
Elizabeth Cowne and Brahm Norwich
ISBN 0 85473 267 5

32. Redefining the Comprehensive Experience
Clyde Chitty (ed.)
ISBN 0 85473 280 2

33. The National Curriculum
Denis Lawton and Clyde Chitty (eds.)
ISBN 0 85473 294 2

34. Girls and Computers: general issues and
case studies of Logo in the mathematics
classroom
Celia Hoyles (ed.)
ISBN 0 85473 306 X

35. Training for School Management: lessons
from the American experience
Bruce S. Cooper and R. Wayne Shute
ISBN 0 85473 307 8

36. Looking, Making and Learning:
art and design in the primary school
Anthony Dyson (ed.)
ISBN 0 85473 312 4